The
LION HEART
WARRIOR

The LION HEART WARRIOR

YOUR PATH TO POTENTIAL, PURPOSE AND POWER

GEORGE A. WEHBY II

LIBERTY HILL PRESS

Liberty Hill Press
2301 Lucien Way #415
Maitland, FL 32751
407.339.4217
www.libertyhillpublishing.com

Printed in the United States of America.

ISBN-13: 978-1-6305-0101-3

CONTENTS

ACKNOWLEDGEMENTS

First and foremost, I want to thank my Lord and Savior Jesus Christ. This is your book my Lord and all credit for its writing belongs to you and the inspiration of Holy Spirit. May God the Father be glorified in this endeavor. Second, I need to thank my wife Jeanne Wehby for tolerating the time away while writing it. Thank you for being the best wife ever and for being so understanding. You are my inspiration.

Next, I need to thank my kids; Bailey, Emma, Mary and Tryce. You guys are my blessing and legacy. May you continue to follow the Lord faithfully all of your days. Next, I must thank my editing team Pastor Chris DeGreen, Barry Rhea, Dr. Andy Maddux, Scott Mayer, Beth Kellogg and Colton Blackburn, you guys are the best.

Thank you to all my students and friends for reading this manuscript in its development and for offering all the much needed suggestions along the way. Thank you for being iron that sharpens iron. May God bless all your Areas of Operation to His Glory!

INTRODUCTION

This adventure all started when I made the decision to read through the book of Ephesians everyday for 21 days straight. At the time, I was attending a congregation that conducted 21 days of prayer and fasting event. During these 21 days, those committed to the process would set aside one hour a day to pray and fast food, media or some important aspect of their life to focus on God. In addition to the prayer and fasting, I decided to add a study component to my devotion. I committed myself to reading through the book of Ephesians 21 times.

On the 17th day of my 21 day commitment, the Lord laid on my heart the book before you. During this revelation, my mind started racing about all the frustrations we experience in our lives. In that moment, it became apparent that the book of Ephesians provided the perfect roadmap for victory in all areas of life.

On the 18th day of my 21 Day commitment, I began to write what you are about to read. Over the course of the next year, I would continue to read the book of Ephesians in its entirety every time I would work on the book. Not one sentence was written or period placed, without me having read Ephesians cover-to-cover first. As you can imagine, the process was tedious and time consuming, but so very worth it. It is important to understand that the information that follows is gathered from the entire council of God's word and not just from the book of Ephesians. The Lord used my study of Ephesians to inspire the information in this book. As I continued to write it out, I felt it was a good idea to consult Ephesians prior to any of those efforts.

Whether you decide to read this book in its entirety or not, know that you can use it as a reference guide and visit the section you need more work in. Our battle for purpose is an ongoing reality and we will have moments of strength and moments of weakness. May God bless your journey and speak to you as you explore what it means to be a Lionheart Warrior. To God be all the Glory!

SECTION I
FOUNDATION

CHAPTER 1
LIFE ALTERING DISCOVERY

I t always seemed like something was missing. From a very early age, I felt as though I was always on the edge of discovering some revelation in life, but never seemed to grasp it and was always left disappointed when the dust settled. As humans, we are creatures of purpose. We are creatures in need of meaning. Unfortunately, we wander around on this planet aimlessly trying to figure out why any of this effort is worth it. I do not know about you, but I found myself exhausted and numb to it all. Do not get me wrong, some seasons of life were exciting and joyous, but they always seemed to default back to the emptiness I mentioned. In the earlier parts of my life, the quest to satisfy that longing drove everything I did and at some level still drives me today. The only difference now is, I know my purpose and why I was so hungry for it before. Understanding this has made all the difference in my life moving forward.

When undertaking to write a book like this one, it is important to get the first chapter right. To be completely honest, this first chapter was by far the hardest to get right. I wanted to capture my reader's attention early on, so that they were more incentivized to read into the later chapters where the good stuff resides. It is my firm belief that the contents of this book have the power to change lives. I know that may sound cliché and cheesy, but it is the absolute truth. It is my mission to give those individuals who take the time to read this book, insight into their purpose and how it drives their identity and sense of significance. I know what you may be thinking, what makes this book any different than the tens of thousands written before? The short answer is nothing—and everything, at the same time. You see, I think we all suffer from the same ailments in life. I think the issues I discuss is inherent in all of us. For the most part, I think some of us either hide it better or compensate for it more. However, there is a third group who have actually overcome it. It is here, where I want us to go in this book. The actual overcoming of our problem.

As I mentioned earlier, I struggled with this longing of something more out of life. It manifested at an early age with me striving to seek the approval of others. I was a slave to "people pleasing." As a child, I would go out of my way not to get in any trouble or even get in "the grown-ups" way. This compensational attitude made me a "good kid" when it came to all the parents, but it was based in fear, not in wanting to do the right thing. Unfortunately, my issue did not stop at people pleasing, it evolved into feelings of inadequacy that even still attempt to rear their head to this very day. At that time, there was not an interaction I found myself in where I felt as though I belonged. I was an imposter. My sense of inadequacy manifested itself in schoolwork, social interactions and especially in athletic pursuits.

Performance anxiety was always a real problem of mine. No matter how well I was at a sport, I always felt as if I was on the verge of a catastrophic failure. My fear of failing led to me out right avoiding certain situations where I was too evenly matched with an opponent. If we were even remotely close in skill set, thoughts of quitting or not even trying my best, were plentiful. I was a poor performance time bomb waiting to explode. The problem was most people had no idea this was my issue. Generally, I did quite well in most areas of my life, so there was no real reason to approach them with me. It was a silent struggle I chose to deal with alone. Looking back, I am thankful for all the negative feelings, thoughts and issues I had as a young man, because they pushed me in the directions my life took. They drove me to find my true purpose and not to settle for some sort of inferior model.

In my pursuit for purpose and meaning, I lived "many lives." During my early twenties and thirties, I had the opportunity to be a part of activities and professions people fantasize about and Hollywood makes movies about. My childhood inadequacies drove me to join the Marine Corps, guard the President of the United States, become a police officer, work as a Federal Air Marshal for the Department of Homeland Security, teach Firearms and tactics for a State Department Private Military Contractor, host a TV show, and earn black belts in numerous martial arts. I do not tell you this to brag, but to express that I tried a great deal of things to bring meaning to my life, and all of them left me wanting more. This all dates back as far as I can remember.

Like most little boys growing up, I always wanted to be a super hero. I wanted a life of adventure defined by courage and danger. During childhood, my play was consumed with quests, competitions and elements of struggle. Typical of little boys, I loved getting into "mischief." I found a way to turn everything into battles of pushing, pulling, striving and conquering. Even my childhood prayers were focused on asking God to grant me super powers like all the cartoon characters I watched on Saturday morning TV. Wanting to be just like them, I would pretend to be in all kinds of scenarios and fights against evil bad guys. To me, super heroes seemed to have true purpose and I wanted to have the same. They all had amazing abilities, skills and what seemed like rock solid confidence. To me, they represented what an ideal man looked like.

As the years passed, my desire to be something more than myself did not go away, it only evolved. I went from wanting to be like super heroes to super soldiers. During my super soldier phase, I played with toy action figures. As part of my play, I figured out how to take the action figures apart and mix up their body parts to make new and unique ones, that better represented me. I was obsessed with being a soldier and possessing all the skills that went into that. My dream was to one day grow up to have their huge muscles, amazing skills and tough guy attitudes. Then, I would be feared and respected.

Not being satisfied with just playing with action figures led to all the neighborhood kids wanting to dress up and "play war" every weekend. We all would fantasize about fighting in mighty battles while crawling in the mud and wading through chest deep water in nearby creeks.

Like all boys around that time of life, I eventually moved into puberty and discovered all the problems associated with that. My biggest struggles during that time were the feelings of insecurity and longing to hurry and grow up to be just like the characters I saw in action movies. These characters did not seem to be insecure at all; characters who seemed to be everything I wanted to be; characters played by actors such as Sylvester Stallone, Arnold Schwarzenegger and Steven Seagal. These guys were incredible. Their characters were unstoppable and prepared for any trouble that came their way. There was no bad guy big enough or strong enough which they could not handle. I wanted nothing more than to be just like them. I wanted all the confidence that came with that.

> *At the time, little did I know this internal desire to measure up, to be the man of action, would consume and haunt me all the way into my adult life.*

At the time, little did I know this internal desire to measure up, to be the man of action, would consume and haunt me all the way into my adult life. My quest for true significance, purpose and that burning desire to be "the guy," would not ever go away. It consumed my every step no matter what I accomplished, no matter what title I earned and no matter what challenge I conquered. It would not be silenced. Since my early childhood, I struggled with the burning questions: Will I be strong enough? Will I be tough enough? Do I have what it takes?

As the years passed, after some big milestone or accomplishment was made, my sense of longing and drive would temporarily be satisfied, but would always return. The feelings of confidence and purpose would always fade reuniting me with those same feelings of inadequacy and insecurity once again. Eventually, after having had enough, I wanted to be rid of them once and for all. My search for significance became very intentional. I would find a way to be free from this bondage of self-doubt and dissatisfaction. Those burning questions of purpose propelled me to find the answer. They sent me on my journey— a journey of self-discovery and a quest to understand the source of my lifelong internal desire.

This journey led to the discovery of what I call the Lionheart Warrior.

On the surface, the term Lionheart Warrior seems comical, like something from fantasy or folklore. Maybe some sort of cartoon character or comic book hero we grew up with—perhaps a medieval knight in a children's story book, but definitely not something to actually strive to become. I chose the term Lionheart Warrior, because it seemed to encapsulate all that I discovered.

Before we get to far ahead of ourselves, it is important to properly define terms and the ideas that drive them. I need to start by taking the term "Lionheart Warrior" and breaking it down, so we can lay the foundation for fleshing out this identity concept.

The term "Lionheart" is a title most often associated with bravery and courage. For example, in the middle ages, the term Lionheart was given to King Richard I of England. He was nicknamed Richard, the Lionheart for his exploits as a great warrior and military leader during the Crusades. He received this designation for displaying lion-like attributes in his approach to fighting in the Holy land.

Like with King Richard, men throughout history have been connected with attributes found inherent in predatory animals. The lion being one of the most popular ones, because they are well known for being courageous and ferocious beasts that possess very few natural predators. They are royal in stature, proud and lethal when engaged in combat. Capable of becoming extremely dangerous in a blink of an eye, lions have a mystique about them of being cool, calm and collected until it is time for them to act. If they are focused in on a prey, there are very few things that will stand in their way. In the wild, the sight of a lion invokes fear in the heart of most creatures. Lions exude the perfect balance of strength and grace.

"A lion, which is mighty among beasts And does not turn away from any;"
Proverbs 30:30 NKJV

Throughout human history, the lion has fascinated and inspired mankind from all walks of life. Their ferocity and courageousness have captivated countless warriors in their preparation for battle. Fighters from all over the world have aspired to imitate the lion and somehow tap into their fearlessness to overcome insecurity and an overwhelming fear of death. In some cultures, as a right of passage, men were required to undergo a confrontation with the beast to be accepted in the tribe.

Unfortunately, my personal experience with an actual lion is rather limited. A close friend of mine tells a story of a personal encounter he and his small daughter had with a lion. While touring a wildlife exhibit many years ago, he and his daughter made their way to the large cat display. The area had numerous cages housing the cats. These caged enclosures allowed a few of the lions the freedom to move about. In the center of this enclosure, about 30 yards away from where they were standing, some of the lions were lying down sunbathing. For added security, the enclosure provided double layer fencing which allowed visitors to get within about five feet of the animals. Being that the lions were resting and not really moving about, there was no real need to be alarmed and my friend's small daughter stood with her hands on the outer fence observing them. Since not much was going on in the cage, my friend became momentarily distracted. When all of a sudden, out of the corner of his eye, he caught a quick flash of movement from the center of the enclosure. In a blurred streak of tan, a lioness came tearing full speed toward his daughter. In what he describes as half a heartbeat, the lioness shot across the enclosure like she was fired out of a cannon. The speed at which she covered the distance was unbelievable. Before he could even flinch, the animal came to a screeching halt dead in front of his daughter, gaze fixed and locked on her tiny frame. Quite naturally, he quickly snatched her into his arms realizing the gravity of what had just happened. A truly life altering experience with a lion.

Stories like the one above are why warriors favor the lion as an inspiration to emulate. They act decisively and without fear. They know who they are and what they are about. The lion is a great example of courage and direction for us to follow.

In an effort to examine this type of courage and resolve, I want you to imagine for a minute that you are a young man born into an African tribe hundreds of years ago. You have finally come of age and it is now time for you to take your place in the tribe. Your entire youth has been spent observing the hunter warriors who came before you. You have witnessed them walk the path you are now on. You have looked up to them and listened to all their glorious stories with excitement and wonder.

Growing up, you imagined yourself eventually walking in their footsteps. As an up-and-coming man in your tribe, you asked those same type questions I mentioned earlier. Am I worthy? Do I have what it takes?

Continuing our train of thought, I want you to imagine that in order to continue in your tribe, you must actually prove your worth. You are required to undergo a test of manhood. Just like all those that came before, you have an obligation to carry on the mantle of warrior-hood for your people. You must prove yourself in battle—that you have courage, strength and valor. You must be convincing. You must walk the path, same as those who came before you. You must kill a lion.

That's right, you must hunt down, confront and corner one of these mighty beasts. You must go toe-to-toe, head-to-head with a killing machine. Not only must you confront it, but you must engage it in combat. You must kill the Lion.

Can you imagine the anxiety, fear and torment you would experience leading up to this event? How would you be able to handle it? Would you even try? Imagine the type of person it would take to do this. Imagine all it would require. In order to rise to the occasion, you would need a lion in your heart bigger than the one you were about to face. It would take a true warrior.

DEFINING THE WARRIOR

Throughout my entire life, I have always obsessed with being a warrior. Warriors possessed all the things I was looking for. They had purpose, direction and a game plan to take on any challenge before them. A true warrior didn't suffer from insignificance, they were always on mission and ready to fight.

"Warrior" is a title given to individuals designated with putting up a fight or engaging in acts of warfare. Warriors are select individuals tasked with bearing arms for a cause. From the beginning of time, warriors have helped shape the cultures of human history. They have represented the best and the worst in mankind. The concept of the "warrior" is at the heart of our search for significance.

These select individuals in a culture are trained in all the necessary skills and strategies of warfare. In order to protect their people, they must learn to operate individually and as part of a larger group. They have to display strength, courage and knowledge in war fighting. Their skill sets are honed over time and need to meet certain set criteria. Through proper training, the warrior develops higher levels of skill to exceed that of their enemy. As protectors and providers for their people, warriors are held in the highest regard in their society. What was true of warriors in the past, is just as true today.

In order to understand the term Lionheart Warrior better, we must tie all of this together. For our journey, we must not only identify what it means to be a Lionheart Warrior, but why it's so important.

Our journey is going to require not only our intellectual understanding of the concept, but a spiritual understanding as well. Like all warriors of the past, there is a deep-rooted spiritual component necessary. It cannot be ignored that there is a driving force inside warriors to transcend the natural order of things. A driving force of purpose which simply cannot be explained away by natural developments in human cultures. It's something beyond; something drawing, prompting and beckoning to unimaginable heights. Something that can only be described as other-worldly—a siren call from the heavenly realms. A call from a cosmic King. A Call From the King of Kings.

In the book of *Revelation*, Jesus, the Son of God, is referred to as the Lion of the tribe of Judah. He is described as a powerful Warrior King, who will return from Heaven and set things right in all of creation. He is a Divine King who is foretold to rally His people and defeat all His enemies. Bringing redemption and vindication to the world, He comes leading an angelic army that will secure final victory over dark forces. A victory which will be the culmination of a war that has stretched across all of space and time—a war that started from the very beginning.

God's word describes battles fought in this protracted war in ways that cannot be understood by natural minds. Jesus, Warrior King and the Son of God, secured victory long before His triumphant return foretold in the book of *Revelation*.

Throughout all ages, mankind has engaged in battles which have stretched over every inch of the earth. Fighting has been waged in physical ways and other ways far beyond conventional battlefields and conventional means. Fighting on a whole 'nother level which ultimately manifests itself in the human heart. Therefore, the war we speak of has produced all other wars, then and now.

It is through insight and understanding of this ultra war, we will find the answers to our burning questions. Our eyes will be opened to the meaning of it all. A true sense of purpose will be discovered. The age-old questions of; "who are we", 'why are we here" and "how do we proceed", will be revealed. We will gain new perspective on why we are dissatisfied in life and what can be done about it. This path is laid before us. Our path has been blazed. We simply need to make up our minds and take first steps to follow wherever it leads. Let our journey begin.

Chapter 2
Source of the Problem

"For we do not wrestle against flesh and blood, but against principalities, against powers, against the rulers of the darkness of this age, against spiritual hosts of wickedness in the heavenly places."
Ephesians 6:12 NKJV

Do not be mistaken; we humans are locked into a war. We are not talking about the battles and skirmishes seen in the news. We are talking about another type of fighting, a kind of conflict that has spawned all other wars. This war we speak of has been claiming mass casualties from the beginning of time. A war with many different faces and forms. Forms that go beyond and behind the physical conflicts we are all-too-familiar with.

As mentioned in the previous chapter, I have always had a bent toward fighting, whether it was playing "war" as a child or training for war as a young man, the path of the warrior has always intrigued me. Beside the mental and physical aspects of combat, I have also sensed there was a battle between good and evil, not only in the world around me, but also in the world within me. As if, there were two separate inclinations prompting me toward them. Prior to discovering the LionHeart Warrior, it was hard to distinguish exactly which was the right way. This confusion often caused a mental cold war, that wasn't paralyzing, but would often leave my decisions made with looming feelings of doubt that perhaps I chose wrongly. A spiritual fog of war if you will.

According to the *Bible*, there is an ancient struggle going on in the spiritual realm—a realm not seen by human eyes; a place not fully understood by man. A place where the struggle is with dark forces, powerful beings and demonic strongholds. Entities that operate here are bygone and formidable. These forces wield mighty influence on our world in ways not fully understood. Making their presence felt by fueling all the disagreements, fights and discord we see around us. Entities standing in direct opposition to forces for good. Two opposing sides locked in perpetual combat.

These two sides have conflicting philosophies and world views. This spiritual war is between the Kingdom of God and a kingdom of darkness. Starting at the dawn of time, this war began and continues to go on until to this very day. The fighting has been fierce and constant. Battlefields have been formed and existed on every plain and stage of creation.

Before we get too deep, we need to get some facts straight. Unlike the bed time stories told to kids and those told to adults through Hollywood, this war is not a deadlock between two equal foes trying to offset the balance between good and evil. These are not equal forces struggling for an edge in power. Let's be clear, it is most definitely not a balance between two equal opposing sides. In reality, it is a colossal mismatch. Looking more like an attempted mutiny rather than an all out civil war. The one side never really had a chance. Matter of fact, they more resemble a small child throwing a temper tantrum, than an equal foe. Make no mistake, the Kingdom of God stands unopposed in this war. In an effort to set the stage early on, we need to understand that God and His cause are secure. Despite how bad things on earth seem to appear, He is always sovereign and nothing has ever been beyond His control.

Put quite simply, the Kingdom of God will always be victorious and always come out ahead. Imagine for a moment there is a battle of wills between a parent and their very small child. The only real power a small child has over their parent is their ability to annoy and frustrate them. This frustration can only be possible because the parent cares for and deeply loves the child. If this love did not exist, the parent would just leave the rebellious child to starve and die. Powerless to take care of itself and ignorant of its vulnerability, the child needs the parent and is truly hopeless without them.

In order to best understand the kingdom of darkness, we need to understand its true nature. Our first step is to learn that it is composed of three basic entities. These three entities work together and have varying roles and duties within the kingdom of darkness. At times, these entities are not completely unified in their approach to fighting the war. Each entity has differing self-interests, which can create internal conflicts. It is a cosmic battle of egos. The kingdom of darkness is composed of the Devil, the World System and the Flesh.

For now, let us simply understand that these three entities at times can operate independent of one another or in conjunction. They represent the "enemy" of God's Kingdom. At the end of the day, they all have a bond and share a common goal in that they desire the thwarting and usurping of God's glory. Ultimately, this is their chief interest. They attempt to accomplish this task either directly or indirectly, intentionally or unintentionally. Most of the time, it is done by redirecting glory away from God and toward something else. Often, they seek their own glory out right and unapologetically.

By His very nature, the God of the universe is all about His own glory. After all, God is the creator and sustainer of all things and therefore deserving of such esteem. The enemy is vehemently opposed to this. Giving glory to God is a conflict of interest on their part, for they desire all glory for themselves. Manifested as a cosmic battle of wills, one side of the equation warrants all the glory and the other side does not. One side wants to steal that which inherently belongs to the other.

I know what you may be thinking. That's it? Seriously? That doesn't seem so terrible. It may even seem a bit petty on God's part. All this conflict and turmoil over something so trivial. Herein lies the problem. As we begin to better understand the nature of God, who He is and what He is about, this reasoning starts to make more sense.

Being extremely motivated, the enemy conducts their part with reckless abandon and are extremely focused in their intent. They understand God's nature and know the affront their desire creates. In the efforts to accomplish this end, they know exactly what they are doing and there is nothing off limits in the pursuit of it. They have been perfecting their approach for a very long time.

To better grasp the importance of fighting over glory, we must begin by understanding the concept of the "almightiness" of God. In His essence, He is the end-all be-all of existence. As the sustainer of all things, for Almighty God to lack glory is for Him to cease being what He is. You cannot have the title "Almighty" without all of the glory associated with it. Attempting to take glory away from Him is an attempt to undermine His very essence.

As we start to understand the connection between glory and God, the reasoning behind the enemy's efforts become more clear. By shifting glory from God, the enemy is attacking the very nature of what it hates. By subverting and undermining His glory, it attempts to tear Him down. Basically, any effort to divert glory to anything other than God is to willfully commit cosmic mutiny. If it were possible for glory to be applied to some other being than that which is almighty, well then the "Almighty" isn't truly all mighty.

As part of the spiritual fog of war, we naturally have a hard time comprehending this concept, because of our finite understanding of an infinite truth. Our flesh (one part of the enemy and also known as "self") acts as a filter preventing our understanding. This filter has a built-in arrogance that demands everything must be able to be understood logically or it is automatically accepted as false. In order to move forward, we need to take a look at the enemies individually to get a better grasp of each of their tactics and motivations. Let's start with the most popular, the Devil.

Due to Hollywood's obsession with evil, it is way easier to conceptualize a devil these days. When speaking of the actual Devil, the biggest problem is the fact that reality is far different from the image most of us are familiar with. Making the Devil out to be a gnarly being with horns and hooves is great at selling movie tickets, but horrible at helping us understand his powerful influence in the world.

In eternity past, the archangel, Lucifer (the Devil), created an insurrection in Heaven. Lucifer became proud in his position amongst the other angels in Heaven. He began to covet God's position within Heaven. Lucifer wanted to divert God's glory to himself. According to scripture, the angel Lucifer was possibly the lead worshipper in Heaven. In the heavenly realm, it was most likely his duty and responsibility to head up the glorifying of God amongst the other angels. Being in that role, Lucifer was intimately familiar with the ins and outs of the glorification process established by God. In this assigned role, Lucifer became proud in his purpose and began to take focus allotted for God and shift it toward himself.

Growing more emboldened, Lucifer began to desire the glory and grew tired of it being directed exclusively at God. At this point, he hatched a plan to seize power and overthrow all of Heaven. In his efforts, Lucifer recruited and led away a third of the other angels in Heaven. In their decision to follow, they became fallen angels or demons through banishment. Lucifer became Satan and was ousted from Heaven in a flash of light, along with all his followers.

We do not know exactly how this all went down, the scriptures simply inform that Satan and the demons were all banished to earth. While on earth, they are awaiting their ultimate and final judgment. With the history of Lucifer's fall in mind, understanding the desire to continue its rebellious efforts makes more sense. While awaiting judgment, they are focused on creating as much discord and havoc in creation as possible. Like a bratty child who does not get its way, they continue their mission out of pure hatred for God and His Kingdom. These demonic forces are always plotting and scheming to keep up the fight. In the devil's effort to continue the war, human agencies were corrupted.

Let's take a look at second entity in the enemy triangle, the World System. The "World" or World System is an entity that is comprised of many different factions and associations. It is a human-based entity that is influenced by the dark forces of the heavenly realms. Sometimes referred to as the "spirit of the age" or "World Order", it is the collective philosophical mindset of fallen humanity.

As we get into the concept and role of sin (not following God's plan and purpose of design) and its consequences, we will see how this World System concept got into creation and how it continues to have such a damaging and devastating effect. The World System is a byproduct of sin's entry into God's creation. It has philosophical leanings toward depravity, destruction and chaos against God's will. Imagine a computer system with a virus that looks to undermine the original computer's programming. This alien software is an infection that creates disorder and destruction. Left unchecked, it makes all original uses and designs of the hardware corrupted.

Sinfulness and the human institutions and cultures that get corrupted by sin compose the World System. Sin causes the parts of the system to be hostile toward God's original design. The World System has an agenda to not only withhold God's glory from Him, but to also lift up and glorify anything else in His place. It acts like an autoimmune disease. It attacks itself, this in direct opposition to its original purpose. All its subversions come in millions of different ways, but all are in line with this same satanic agenda. Through the use of discrediting, mocking and outright assaulting the things of God, it pushes the kingdom of darkness' goal forward. By pushing a false narrative, the World System drives forward a "truth" in opposition to the one presented by God. The World System can be seen in all cultures, medias and interactions of human society. The system takes forms in all human interactions outside those instituted by God.

As we come to the last entity making up the enemy, for us, it can be the hardest to swallow and deal with. This due to how close to home it operates. Not surprisingly, it is an enemy that exists in our own hearts. Cunning and crafty, this enemy is in a league all its own. Often referred to in the Bible as the "Self, Flesh, Natural man" or "Old Man," it is an entity attached to us at our conception. A product of humanity's fallen state, the Flesh was brought to us by our ancestor and the very first human, Adam.

The Flesh is our fallen fleshly nature and its sole agenda is self-seeking glorification. Being the master of self-centeredness, our sinful nature wants nothing more than to be served. Even when engaged in activities that could be labeled "noble" or "good," our nature will lift and prop itself up. Seeking credit for everything and anything, it will shift blame away from itself at the first sign of failure. A pinnacle of arrogance and insecurity, the flesh knows no bounds in pursuit of personal glory. At the height of delusion, our fallen nature will paint itself in whatever light best serves itself and its interests.

As an example of this, while struggling with my sense of insignificance and purposelessness, I found my greatest trouble was in the area of humility. I could not get past the belief that I somehow possessed the answer and would ultimately be the one to figure out the solution to my problems. Often times unconscious, I seemed to deny, ignore or even explain away any revelation that my problem resided within me affecting how I saw things. It had to be some external problem which needed identifying and eradicating, instead of something inherent within me.

In no way wanting to make light of this truth, it is critical we understand that we all possess this nature and it has powerful influence. It is inherent within us and we are born a slave to it. Our flesh sets us against and on the opposite side from the Kingdom of God. We are born in rebellion to Him. The demonic forces, the World System and our fallen nature all work together in this. They are interconnected and operate in conjunction with one another. Whether intentional or unintentional, the Self is set at odds with Almighty God. Keep

> *Whether intentional or unintentional, the Self is set at odds with Almighty God.*

in mind, we are talking exclusively about us as humans in our natural, unchecked state which exists outside the saving grace of God in Christ.

Now I know what you might be thinking, how is that possible? There must be some mistake. I know plenty of people who love God and serve Him. Where do they all fit in?

My follow up questions would look something like this:

Are they really loving God and serving Him? Or do they just think they are?

What if they are really loving the god of their own making, a god of their own design?

Are they serving Him from a pure place of humility or perhaps as some sort of cosmic genie or divine good luck charm?

Is their god, the God who revealed himself to man as laid out in His word? Is He the same God who lays out His likes, dislikes, plans and purposes in great detail through scripture? Is He the same God who stands on the fact you are either with Him or aligned against Him?

The scriptures are very clear that we are born enemies of God in our mind and that *no one* seeks after God; that there are none righteous and pleasing to Him. God made it very clear prior to rescuing and redeeming His people, we were enemies and alienated from Him. We were fighting for the wrong side. We were living to satisfy our own agenda, desires and personal glory. We were users and abusers of others, things and circumstances pushing our own mini kingdom of Self.

If we were religious at all, it was because we needed to serve a god of our liking. We needed to feel better about our state of being and needed to serve a god of our own creation. One of our own making. One that fit nicely in our box. Even better, we needed to find institutions and maxims to validate our false god. A god that would make us feel good about our situation and the life we lead. This was a god of our mind and this god gave us comfort. In reality, we were just him in disguise— our Flesh lying to us—telling us a story to keep us in slavery to self and keeping us delusional and fighting for the wrong side. In this way, we stayed at odds with Almighty God and opposed to our original design.

Taking all this into account, how can we truly love God and serve Him? Why would He ever want such a vile rebellious creature in His presence? If properly examined, our whole sinful fallen situation seems pretty bleak, depressing and hopeless.

Fear and fret not. Like all stormy days, there is light that pierces the darkness.

There is Good News!

God has a plan. God has always had a plan; a plan that undermines all the enemy while at the same time freeing us from our destructive path. A master plan to return us to our original purpose. A restoration plan to re-instate our ability to reflect glory as His image bearers. A plan to be at peace with Him for all eternity.

There Is Hope!

Almighty God has provided the way to reunite us. He has provided the way to reconcile us. He has provided the way to re-instate us. He has provided the way to resurrect us to a greater status than our ancestor Adam had before. We will no longer be enemies fighting against Him, but warriors fighting for Him. This redemptive plan will come at great personal cost. It will require laying down our arms. It will require our complete surrender and betrayal to our former masters. It will require confession of our crimes and the letting go of our rebellion once and for all.

It's time for the Revolution.

CHAPTER 3
THE MISSION IMPOSSIBLE

"**H**ouston, we have a problem!"

Those words were transmitted from the damaged Apollo 13 Moon Lander to NASA from outer space. The Apollo 13 mission to the moon ran into some unforeseen issues while trying to make the very dangerous trek to the lunar surface. The mission was going according to plan, that is until they heard a loud bang on the spacecraft. At first, the crew thought it was not that big of a deal, well until they started to lose power and run out of air. For the crew in space, it was a very bad situation that was only getting worse.

As the astronaut crew began to realize the extent of their problem, it became very clear that if they did not fix it quickly, they would be out of time and die thousands of miles from home. Communicating with the scientists back on earth over the radio, they all began working through the details. This was only possible, because some of the smartest individuals at that time worked tirelessly to solve this deadly problem. Given all the restraints, everyone involved brainstormed for hours trying to figure out ways to bring the crew home safely.

In order to better understand the crews available options in space, NASA scientists and engineers ended up creating an exact replica of the Apollo 13 back on earth to work with. By making the replica, they wanted to figure out a solution using only the tools, items and objects accessible to their crew stranded in space. Since they were running out of breathable air, their problem was compounded, not to mention they were practically freezing to death out there with no heat.

Obviously, the odds were heavily stacked against the Apollo 13 crew. Their situation looked extremely bleak and most everyone in the world felt the task of rescuing them was next to impossible. Through amazing perseverance, all those involved worked the problem and figured out a way to get the crew home safely.

During this whole ordeal, the most intense moment came when the rescue plan was fully underway and the crew had to go silent for a few hours upon re-entry into the earth's atmosphere. Every re-entry had a standard time of communication black out while descending back through the atmosphere; however, when the Apollo 13 space-craft was re-entering, that prescribed time of silence was unintentionally over-extended to everyones dismay. This protracted silence left all those involved fearful of the worst possible outcome. Every extra second over that allotted time was understood to mean catastrophic failure and that the crew had most likely been tragically killed.

During that time, every extra second left everyone on the edge of their seats dreading the worst. As the world waited in anticipation, all hope of the crew's survival started to falter. Then out of nowhere, with a crack of the radio, the silence was broken as the crew signaled the all clear and that they were safe. All those waiting in anticipation around the world burst with joy as word was announced the rescue was successful.

They had pulled it off. NASA rescued their guys with a near impossible plan. Through quick thinking and ingenuity, the crew used the resources on hand to fix their problem and save their own lives. It was a mission almost impossible.

Like the flight crew of Apollo 13, we too, have a problem — a very dangerous problem. We too, have experienced catastrophic failure. We are in dire straights and running out of time. However, unlike the crew, our problem is not a mechanical one. Unfortunate for us, our problem cannot be solved by NASA ingenuity. Despite all our know-how and superior intelligence, we do not possess the capabilities to save ourselves.

Quite simply, our problem goes much deeper and is way more complicated, because...

We ARE the problem.

You see, Our problem is ourselves —humans that is. We have created and continue to create a major problem for ourselves. Unlike the astronauts in Apollo 13, we are not capable of helping ourselves by taking life saving steps. To be honest, we do not even fully understand how serious our problem really is, much less how to go about fixing it.

Despite all of this, there is good news. God saw our problem coming and it did not catch Him by surprise. Thankfully, He is never taken by surprise. The Almighty God of the universe knows all things and sees all things. He always has and He always will. Along with being all knowing, His ways are always right and true. We must understand that these simple facts about God are key to this, because our true problem is with Him and our relationship with Him. We see this in two major ways.

The first way has to do with our loyalties. Bottom line, we are traitors. Yes, you heard me —traitors. I know this assessment comes off harsh and cuts deep. Trust me, I feel it too, but it's true. We were created to be in relationship with Him. Were were designed to be in fellowship with Him and quite frankly, we are not. Like I said before, we are traitors to the One who created us, traitors to the One who designed us and gave us our purpose. We are dirty rotten traitors. Traitors to God.

> *At the heart of our being, we are self-centered and completely self-absorbed.*

Now do not get me wrong, some of us are a little worse than others, but if you think about it, we are all pretty rotten to the core. It's just that some of us are better at covering it up. We were born and live as rebels and exist in a state of rebellion to our Creator. At the heart of our being, we are self-centered and completely self-absorbed. Anyone being truly honest with themselves will agree that we only really care about ourselves. This fact flies in the face of an all powerful sovereign God, who has ever right to demand complete and utter loyalty. We are either all in or all out when it comes to serving Him. Unfortunately, no matter our level of intent or consciousness, we are against Him and have inadvertently declared war by our choosing ourselves over Him in rebellion.

Since we are locked in all-out revolt, we are stuck fighting for a lost cause and on the side doomed to failure. To make matters worse, we are fighting for the side of entities that actually hate us and just wants to use us. Whether we meant to do it or not, we are fighting for the kingdom of darkness. To be more specific, we fight for our own kingdom —a kingdom of Self. Our self-centric kingdom is in direct opposition to God's Kingdom.

Our alignment with the kingdom of darkness comes at a price. A price of separation and isolation from our design and purpose. An inherent disconnect we experience in all areas of our existence. One that testifies to our rebellion and break with the Creator.

As a needed reminder, it is not a war of equal sides. Our kingdom is a destined loser, which is plagued with that hardship and despair. We are wrapped up in that life filled with delusion and confusion. An existence wrapped in sin and separation from God's blessing. This is our fallen state. That is where we are, or at least where we use to be. Rebellious. Throwing a cosmic temper tantrum, demanding the universe bend to our will.

If I were to reverse the roles and I were God, I would not put up with such arrogance, entitlement and disgusting behavior. I would snap my fingers scrapping it all and start all over again. I would build a new, better world, with new and better people, ones who appreciate all I do for them. A people who will be my representatives and who are passionately in love with my rule.

That's what I would do.

Well believe it or not, that is exactly what God did.

Well ... kinda.

Similar to those NASA scientists, God hatched a plan to rescue us. He created a plan to fix our dangerous problem. Wanting to prevent our destruction, He devised a plan which would punish our insubordination, while at the exact same time provide a way for us to be rescued and redeemed. Unlike the space crew once trapped in Apollo 13, God's plan could only be pulled off 100% by Himself. He had to be the one to do it. In our fallen state, we were incapable. Not only were we incapable, we were unwilling.

God's plan, though brilliant, came at the highest cost. Though ingenious, His plan was extremely brutal. God provided a way to exact His righteous judgment as sovereign Lord, while simultaneously displaying His magnificent grace and love. As holy and righteous God, He did not overlook our rebellion. Here in lies the crux of the issue. Ultimately, we had to be punished for our rebellion. Since God is holy and righteous, His character required vindication. He had declared the consequences of insurrection to His throne. The consequences were exact. He always binds Himself to His declarations and will always uphold them. For the outcome of sin is the punishment of death.

Here in lies the conundrum. God desired to save His people and execute justice at the same time. He desired to show mercy and enact vengeance together. Being that God is God and can do all things, He enacted a plan. A plan that would accomplish both of these perfectly. One that at no point would sacrifice or give up His glory. He enacted vengeance and mercy simultaneously.

In a plan that only He could devise, God accomplished this holy vindication while at the same time redeeming and transforming us rebels into His new righteous army. A fighting force of pure and loyal troops; a royal tribe of warriors for His eternal glory. In the biggest turning point in human history, God pulled off a miracle like no other. One that defied all odds and flew in the face all conceivable expectations.

Based on His love, He decided to save us from destruction, while at the same time maintaining integrity and not lowering His standard of perfection. We could not just simply change our minds and therefore change our sides. We could not just simply say we were sorry and everything be forgotten and forgiven. That would have still violated His holy righteousness. Punishment had to be levied.

We had to pay for our crimes. The sins could not just be swiped away and everyone just move on. This would have violated His integrity and have required the Almighty to cease being almighty. God would have had to value His mercy above His justice. He would have had to become a liar and a hypocrite. Quite simply, God held Himself to His own standard.

So, what was His way of accomplishing all of this? A way that satisfied His justice and kept His glory intact? A way that accomplished both His justice and mercy? A way that demonstrated His perfect love? A miraculous way? The only Way?

Jesus.

The King of the universe devised and initiated a plan to rescue us from our fallen state and bring us back to His Kingdom. It was a plan like no other — a glorious rescue plan that accomplished all His divine requirements — a plan that used a man to get it done. Not just any man, it took a special man. A man like all the others, but at the same time, like no other. God threw in a twist.

That man was Almighty God Himself.

In order to get the job done, God the Father sent His one and only Son, Jesus. He became like us in order to rescue us. God became like us. He took on our nature, but without sin. Jesus experienced our life, the

> *Jesus experienced our life, the troubles, traumas, joys and triumphs, the love and the hate — the human experience in all its essence.*

troubles, traumas, joys and triumphs, the love and the hate — the human experience in all its essence. In doing this, He decided to redeem us rebels on a spiritual, mental and physical level, by taking on all our crimes as if they were His own. Despite being fully innocent, He took them all.

He was our representative.

He became like us.

God became man and dwelt among us.

Jesus lived as we lived and walked as we walked. He lived the life we should have — the perfect life, a life of righteousness. Despite His complete submission to God the Father's will, He chose to suffer the punishment He had not earned. He endured the punishment we deserved. He took on all the pain and suffering of righteous judgment, all so we would not have to. In so doing, Jesus received the full measure of justice. He endured the full mantle of God's judgment and set us free.

Free and clear.

Our debt paid.

Declared innocent.

Unlike those rebels He saved, He was as loyal as one could possibly be to the Kingdom of God. He never aligned against it, subverted authority or took up arms against the crown. Yet, Jesus took the punishment. He endured it and became the object of almighty holy vengeance. Why? Why would He go through all of that?

One reason and one reason only — love. Love of His people. Love for those who hated Him. Love God has for His creation.

It broke His heart to see them lost. It broke His heart to see them fallen. It broke His heart to see them without hope waiting for eternity without Him. Taking the initiative, He stepped into the gap and made a way. He had the perfect fix to restore them all to Himself.

The King of glory sent Himself as His Son.

He sent Jesus on this fatal mission to bring us home, back to where we belong.

There was no other way, to conduct His mission, Jesus had to taste death. Not just any death — a gruesome death — a violent death at the hands of the very ones He came to save. The death of a condemned criminal.

Unlike the criminals that came before Him, Jesus death on that cross was on a whole other level — a supernatural level; a compounded level of material and spiritual. He took ALL the punishment. Not just one man's punishment, but the punishment for all the world. In that one moment in time, all the accumulated punishments of humanity were combined and channeled onto Him. Manifested into the act of being beaten and hung on a Roman cross.

At that fateful moment of crucifixion, a supernatural link happened. All our pain and suffering were compounded. All our fear, guilt and shame were connected and infused onto Him. Jesus embodied our misery and sin. All of it; all at once. Only God could receive such a blow and only a man could experience such a blow.

In order for this to work, He had to be one of us. It had to be one our own. Both were absolutely necessary. Only Jesus could do it.

It was done.

It was completed.

It was finished.

The Son of God had taken it all, once and for all, never to be done again. Death on a cross. The cost and price for our redemption was complete. Unearned and undeserved. Paid. Receipt delivered. The most selfless act ever conceived or demonstrated was realized. Nothing even comes close. How could it?
Justice and mercy united. Sacrifice accomplished.

A sacrifice that could never be earned. A sacrifice that could never be merited, bought, negotiated or strived for. Given freely.
The body of Jesus was laid to rest in a tomb of silence —a complete communication blackout. Like those waiting for news from the Apollo 13 spacecraft wondered: Did the rescue operation work? Was the payment enough to save us? Was all the suffering and struggle experienced for nothing?

One day goes by. Nothing. Silence. Still He lay in the tomb.

Two days go by. Nothing. Silence. Still there.

Apollo 13 can you read us?

Apollo 13 please respond.

Apollo 13 can you read?

Then the miracle occurred. Early on the third day, the incredible happened. The physically impossible took place. Jesus' once shattered body was gone —vanished without a trace. His corpse nowhere to be found. All that was left in an open grave were the linens He was buried in. Neatly folded as if waiting to be collected. What could that mean? Did it work? Were we freed?

On this third day, Almighty God conducted the second half of His divine rescue operation. Defying all the laws of nature and logic, Jesus was made alive. Resurrected. Brought back. Returned. And made whole. Victorious! Appearing triumphantly to His people proclaiming the good news of their redemption. He revealed the incredible truth of their forgiveness. They were freed!

We are free!!!

Through this amazing act of mercy and love, Almighty God accomplished His redemptive plan. He made the way to forgiveness for us rebels. He created a path for our restoration. He paved the road to a new life under the authority of a new kingdom, under a new king, the King of kings and Lord of lords, His Son, Jesus Christ.

In order to receive this amazing grace, His only requirement was for those insurgent, renegade and rebellious warriors to admit their crimes, confess their sinful ways, reject their former actions and receive the gift of Jesus. The gift of redemption and salvation, eternal life to be received through faith, through trusting belief in who He is and what He had done for them. The payment accomplished in Christ. In doing this, we pledge an undying faithfulness to His authority and a rejection of our former path, our former life of sin.

During this process, Almighty God created in us redeemed warriors, a new spirit. Our old Self had been unified to the Son on the cross — killed — dismantled and defeated. We warriors became new. Almighty God indwell them. He inhabits our spirit. Jesus lives in us, insuring fidelity to Himself and His crown. We become something different. We become like the Son, who saved us.

This is the only way. This is the only option Almighty God set forth to accomplish the mission of bringing us home; the mission of rescuing, restoring and redeeming these once rebellious warriors from the kingdom of darkness. This was and is His secret weapon. This is His solution to all our problems. This is the foundation to all our triumphs in this life. This is the way to our being made right now and in the life to come.

As warriors, we inherently want to fight. We want to go to war. We are itching for a cause and an objective to accomplish. Left to our own selves, we will choose the wrong path. We will go the wrong way. Thankfully, our creator provided the way to make us right with Him and the power to follow it. Jesus provided and provides the ability for us to live the life we couldn't have lived otherwise. He provides not only the plan, but also the means to which we can execute it. He empowers his new warriors to become lions. He forms the substance of their new being to fulfill His design. They are given a new heart. A heart of a lion. A lion come to reside in their heart.

The LION.

God's LION.

Jesus, the lion of the tribe of Judah, comes and dwells inside of us. It's up to us to realize it. It's up to us to get out of the way and let God's lion roar. His Spirit. His Being. The Spirit of His Son. The indwelling empowerment that saves. His presence inhabits the believer. This person empowers the new creature. All accomplished in this once rebellious warrior, through belief and trusting faith. A faith that consumes and transcends the intellect. A faith that saves through the power of Almighty God's amazing grace in His Son.

This moving faith leads the new warrior to fight a new fight. To fight in a new way. The way to discovering and understanding the path into the purposes of God. A purpose of taking the fight to the enemy and their kingdom of darkness.

God's way.

The only way.

Have you received the King's pardon? Have you pledged your loyalty to Him? Have you put your trust in the One who saves?

The time is now, for the days are evil.

Choose this day, whom you will serve!

CHAPTER 4

DESTROYING DELUSION

"For which of you, intending to build a tower, does not sit down first and count the cost, whether he has enough to finish it —"
Luke 14:28 NKJV

The day I went off to boot camp was a milestone in my life. Up to the point when I got off that bus, it didn't seem real. Even after all the signing of forms, raising of right hands and the repeat after me stuff, it didn't truly seem real. It wasn't until we pulled into that famous parking lot late that night, that it all started to set in. I had arrived at The United States Marine Corps Recruit Depot in Parris Island, South Carolina.

At first, my decision to enlist in the Marines was just a crazy idea made by an adventurous teenager. It was all just an extreme initial step in my new journey of adulthood. What I had decided to do wasn't real in my mind, until the moment I found myself standing on those famous yellow footprints. Up to that point, there was a part of me that felt this was all just a dream.

This dream of mine would soon became a dynamically aggressive whirlwind of chaotic shuffling and screaming of Drill Instructors, marking the beginnings of my personal transformation. Now at that hour, it was all too real. The commitment I made a few short hours ago was being realized, whether I was ready for it or not. Thrust headlong into becoming a United States Marine, I was now all-in.

We as human beings are all about status. We are all about knowing exactly where we stand in our many areas of life. Whether its family, friends, career or athletic activity, we want to know how we measure up. It's a great motivator. We are looking for validation and approval. If you claim you are above all those things, chances are high you are claiming that because you want to be seen as the person who is "above all of this."

The fact that we as humans are constantly looking and striving to see how we measure up is nothing new; our sense of approval dates back to the very beginning. It dates back to the fall of humanity; going way back to the interactions of our first parents, Adam and Eve. I know what some of you may be thinking, that story isn't meant to be taken literally. Well, all I know is, the story explains a whole lot about why we do the things we do.

> *"And when the woman saw that the tree was good for food, and that it was pleasant to the eyes, and a tree to be desired to make one wise, she took of the fruit thereof, and did eat, and gave also unto her husband with her; and he did eat. And the eyes of them both were opened, and they knew that they were naked; and they sewed fig leaves together, and made themselves aprons. And they heard the voice of the Lord God walking in the garden in the cool of the day: and Adam and his wife hid themselves from the presence of the Lord God amongst the trees of the garden. And the Lord God called unto Adam, and said unto him, Where art thou? And he said, I heard thy voice in the garden, and I was afraid, because I was naked; and I hid myself."–Genesis 3:6-10 KJV*

It all started with a bad decision. A decision to violate a command from God. It all begins with a failure in preset boundaries. In violating His command, Adam and Eve plunged themselves and all of us after them, into a life of fear, shame, deception and conflict.

The consequence for this infraction was laid out ahead of time by God, and it was severe. Death. Not only physical bodily death, but spiritual death, emotional death, relational death. Death, death, death.

The human race was funneled into an existence of separation at our deepest level; separation from ourselves and our creator. To this day, the separation is manifested throughout all areas of our lives, from how we relate to each other, the outside world and even within ourselves. Mankind is lost, disconnected, afraid and in perpetual hiding.

This separation translates into to a battle of kingdoms, a cosmic power struggle and all the lengths God went through to redeem us. Despite all of that, there are areas of our lives where we continue experiencing fear, shame, deception and conflict at our deepest level. Areas affecting our day-to-day, moment-by-moment interactions. Areas impacting everything we know and care about, including the people we interact with every day. Areas that are in the forefront of our minds. We find ourselves battling this fear, shame, deception and conflict all the time.

All of our choices are shaped at some level by how we are going to be viewed or how our message will be received. Our situation creates an ever-present state of defensiveness in order to counter the fear and shame. Our defensiveness leads to deception in all our interactions, triggering conflict. This chain reaction creates a vicious cycle filtering into all the different areas of our life.

We take all kinds of steps to avoid these issues. We conduct varying levels of deception and manipulation to avoid the fears and potential shame. We create all kinds of false responses, reactions, personalities and explanations to avoid truths exposing our vulnerability and weakness. Like Adam and Eve who came before us, we are naked and afraid, hiding in the bushes attempting to avoid detection. Anyone with the slightest sense of introspection will find this to be true. I do not care how "confident," "secure" or "together" you seem to be, by nature we all suffer from this same ailment. Trouble is, some are just better at hiding it than others. This is our default state. It's our personal defense mechanism, a kind of spiritual and mental habit, a byproduct and holdover of an existence fighting for the kingdom of darkness.

Most of the time it comes down to us liking the idea of being made right by our new allegiance to the King, but our internal lives rarely reflect our new status. Yes, we have been given freedom from darkness by the King of Kings, but we are still locked in prison. The disconnect between the truth of God's provision and how we live our lives, can be seen everywhere. We see our failures. We know our insecurities. We experience the shame and deception they bring. We have a crisis of belief. We love intellectually the idea that we have been freed from our rebellious state by God's provision in His Son, but we live our lives in a much different fashion. This revolution of freedom provided by Jesus should have extended throughout every area of our lives. It should have caused night and day differences within us. Unfortunately, it is simply not the case. We do not see a real difference. Let's be completely honest, for most of us, things haven't really changed at all. Why?

Trust. Belief. Faith.

It's fine and dandy to like the story of what Jesus did. It's fine and dandy, to hear how it empowers us. It's great to think about what life would be like if we actually lived it out, but we don't. We are still living like before. We are still living in rebellion. We are still living in fear, doubt and discouragement. We are still wearing the shame of our inner selves every moment of every day. We are still caught up in the activity of covering up, hiding, manipulating all in an attempt to make others believe we are something we are not.

Let's face it, we are LIARS!

It's harsh, I know. Trust me, it cuts deep within me as well. We are deceptive. We cover up and manipulate. We tell half-truths, if we tell any truth at all. We withhold key information to not be found out or look inferior and inept. We frame and twist things to make our circumstances appear more appealing, more acceptable, more redeemable. We plaster on a fake smile and push through the doubt in hopes it will all get done, whatever that might be. We do not experience true lasting victory.

It does not have to be like this. It does not have to be this way. There is an answer. There is a resolution. There is a remedy to our hang-ups. We have access to true freedom from this fallenness. We have access to the way things ought to be. We have access to the truth, the whole truth, the truth that sets us free. The cost of this freedom is high. It requires an honest assessment of ourselves. It requires a commitment of our entire being. It requires a loss of self. A death to self. A death to the old way. It requires us to go all-in— all the way in. A change of mind. A change of direction. No half stepping. No fence riding. Taking the full plunge. Stripping everything down and surrendering all to the One who made us. Laying down our arms. Laying down our rebellion. Laying down all our dreams and all our desires apart from Him. Laying down our very lives. A true abandonment of self. It requires commitment. It requires a decision.

Once that weighty decision we are talking about is made, something supernatural occurs. Once commitment to the way of the King truly occurs, something extraordinary happens. Once turning from the old and toward Him is done, it all changes. There is a rebirth. A glorious internal transformation begins. We become sealed with His Spirit. There and only there, the path of the Lionheart Warrior begins. In losing it all, we gain His ultimate ALL.

Where are you?

Do you know? Have you experienced the call? Has this happened before in the past and you held something back? Did you ever really fully go all-in? Did you feel the draw only to ignore it or delay?

The day is at hand. Now is the time. Now is the hour to go all-in. Now is the moment for us to become who we are truly designed to be. Now is the time to change our path and surrender to our Sovereign King. Now is the time to truly believe.

Now is your time to fully receive.

SECTION II
BASIC TRAINING

Chapter 5
The Rebirth

It was early spring in 1995. I was fresh out of High School and in the midst of failing out of college. In the hopes of altering the trajectory of my life toward something meaningful, I enlisted in the Marine Corps. Looking for a path that would redefine me, the Marine Corps seemed like the obvious choice. I chose the Marines for the simple fact it seemed to be the most difficult of all the other services.

Grounded in the obsessive desire to become an idealized version of myself, I chose the one that scared me the most. I believed deep down that if I not only graduated, but did well in Basic Training, I would finally rid myself of those childhood insecurities.

Up to that point, all my efforts to alleviate this yearning had failed. I truly counted on my decision to join the Corps as being that missing link. I was sure my obsession would magically be gone the moment I earned the title of Marine.

At that point, I had grandiose ideas of the Marines. They were those soldiers I pretended to be as a child. To me, they were the toughest men I could imagine. They had to be, they were the ones who ran into the fight when others were running away. I had uncles who fought in WWII, friends of my parents who fought in Nam and guys I looked up to who fought in Desert Storm — all Marines.

Needless to say, I had a gambit of examples to pool from; some realistic, some not so realistic. Despite everything, the real-life men I knew had this confidence about them that seemed to be garnered from their time in the Marines. I was convinced of this and desperately wanted what they had. With the aid of Hollywood and a couple of "former Marines" in my life, I set out on a path to solve my issue.

The Corps has a unique way of forging once snotty-nosed, undisciplined boys into hardcore fighting men. They have a well thought out process of development. It is a meticulous system worked out over two centuries of U.S. history. The Corps' process changes these individuals from the inside out; forging mind and body simultaneously.

As a new recruit, you learn to think differently, speak differently, walk differently and be different. It is a complete culture shock. In the course of 13 weeks, a recruit undergoes a minute by minute gauntlet of intense training to tear down the old and lay the foundation for something new. It's a thorough process of stripping down and building up that leaves the recipient changed forever. Through a metaphorical death and rebirth, the individual is transformed. By the time of graduation, you go from one thing to something else completely.

"Therefore if any man be in Christ, he is a new creature: old things are passed away; behold, all things are become new." -2 Corinthians 5:17 KJV

Unlike the Marines' process of development, God's forging of His warriors is perfectly executed. Where the Marines focus only on the physical and mental side of transformation, God's way incorporates every area of a person's life — a complete and total transformation of being.

The Lionheart Warrior's path is one of natural and supernatural death and resurrection — a process of leaving the old way and embracing the new at their center. It's a process incorporating the natural areas of life as well as the spiritual. Change happens primarily on a spiritual level and has a rippling effect to the natural level.

The once rebellious creature is transformed by the Creator into a divinely crafted new creation. God alters us at the deepest level; a level not understandable by the finite mind, but apparent and tangible none the less. Change is felt in all aspects of our existence. It is a process only accomplished at the God level and then realized at our human level. It's a radical transformation that defies material explanation and logic; a stumbling stone to those outside the know.

> *Each of God's warriors are unique and He develops them at different rates and in varying areas of their life.*

God's process incorporates changes at different times and measures. There is no standard path or timeline for change. Each of God's warriors are unique and He develops them at different rates and in varying areas of their life. His goal is the same, but His trajectory varies.

God's process happens over a lifetime. God's training never stops. Graduation is at physical death. The training process is all a part of the goal. God's purpose is in the forming of His warriors. It is all a part of His divine plan. It is the mission to be accomplished. In the Marine Corps, there is a purpose to creating Marines. There is an objective. There are needs to be met. Created for particular roles, there are tasks to be accomplished and duties to be filled. Our purpose is pre-selected and all our training and skill development reflect that purpose.

> *"Blessed be the God and Father of our Lord Jesus Christ, who hath blessed us with all spiritual blessings in heavenly places in Christ: According as he hath chosen us in him before the foundation of the world, that we should be holy and without blame before him in love: Having predestinated us unto the adoption of children by Jesus Christ to himself, according to the good pleasure of his will,*
> *-Ephesians 1:3-5 KJV*

God does an amazing work in His new warrior. The transformative work is incredible — going from rebellious, self-absorbed fighter for the kingdom of darkness to an individual wholly committed to Christ and His kingdom. We are put through a supernatural adoption and regeneration processes. In an instant, the warrior is made like the King. Through an immersion of spirit, we are transformed. Difficult to grasp is the fact of the instantaneousness of it all in the spiritual. At the moment of belief, we are completed at the spiritual level, while also being forged through a lifetime of training. Truly mind melting.

Faith being the catalyst, God accomplishes in the believer the miraculous work in the moment of trusting faith. All accomplished by faith and reliance on the works of the Son. Trust in His rescue operation and no longer in our own efforts at redemption. It's what He did, not what we did, do or will do. Defying human comprehension and understanding, but accomplished nonetheless, we realize through trial, tribulation and a forging of fire that any actions done by us are actually powered and completed by Christ. God wills it and through us accomplishes His purpose. We are a willing vessel of His power. He does it all through us. We are provided everything needed. He has accomplished it all.

As an example, I once heard about a guy living down and out on his luck without a penny to his name. Living paycheck to paycheck, he had very little extra money to go around. Always breaking even, he lived in virtual poverty. Every dime earned was already assigned a bill prior to receiving it. Needless to say, he lived a financially dissatisfied existence. Despite his best efforts, he felt like a slave to his financial circumstance. No matter the effort, he could not improve his station in life because all his time was spent working multiple jobs to make ends meet. There was no extra effort to be made, because there were no spare moments to be had. All options for career change were impossible; therefore, he was stuck with no escape.

Unbeknownst to him, a few years back he inherited a large sum of money from his estranged father. The inheritance was apparently some sort of insurance policy naming him as primary beneficiary. The policy went active the moment his father passed away. The insurance company had trouble locating him since the relationship was severed many years prior.

When he eventually found out about the money, his life changed in an instant. Living all that time under dire financial circumstances; he no longer had to. Unaware of his new state, he was still trapped in poverty despite his status change. Once he was aware, he was transported mentally from despair to hope, from a life of poverty to a life of means, all without any real effort of his own. He needed only to recognize and accept his new state given to him by his father.

Similar to the story of that man, we must fully realize and accept our change in status. We can then start to live out our new status. Until that truth is understood, we will operate under the old belief; our old understanding of self. We will continue struggling and striving to produce benefits that have already been secured. This is the sad state of many warriors today — not understanding the power and being we have become. We live sad, defeated lives.

Having trusted the King, we do not understand the power we are given. We live the old way. It is only through a desire to learn and receive these truths, can we start experiencing the effects and benefits of our new calling and status.

As we proceed through the Lionheart Warrior training, we will start to get a deeper understanding of the truths and empowerment of our new birth. We will better understand our calling, mission and the tools God has provided. The old understanding is heavily ingrained and requires diligence to uproot. In doing that, we will understand our mission and the stakes being played daily. We will experience all the pitfalls and peaks of His process — the process of becoming all we were designed to be. We will learn of our role, and feel the sense of purpose it brings. The time is now. Your time is now!

Our King calls!

Chapter 6
Areas of Operation

As a Brazilian Jiu-jitsu instructor, I have been forced to evolve my teaching strategy over the years. Since Jiu-jitsu is a grappling martial art that requires you to wrap your opponent up like a snake, all the information can be very overwhelming in the details and nuances. You must use your whole body in a coordinated effort to control and trap your opponent. Unlike most other martial arts, Jiu-jitsu has to be tested with 100% resistance for any real skill to develop. That means the training partner is actively trying to counter and thwart everything the student is trying to accomplish. The training is intense and requires a certain level of cardiovascular endurance and agility. Participants are trying to choke and hyper-extend each other's arms and legs in a physical battle of wills. Due to the stressful nature of the training, it translates better to actual fighting than the choreographed moves found in other more popular martial arts.

During the Jiu-jitsu learning phase, you cannot develop skill by trying to understand all the component parts at once. It is just too overwhelming. Each area must be broken down into smaller details, making them easier to grasp. As the student gets the hang of it, more detail is provided and the training becomes more and more complex. This allows the student to see minor successes and eventually put all the parts together as a whole. It is only through dissection of the parts, where you can get a proper understanding of the objectives and pitfalls of the art.

Similar to developing martial arts skill, fighting a war can seem like an impossibly daunting task. As with any serious problem to solve, there are many areas and angles to address and contended with. It, too, can become rather overwhelming. If we do not take the time to truly understand our problem, we can make poor decisions leading to catastrophic results. Every military commander needs missions and objectives to accomplish in order to keep efforts moving forward in the right direction on the battlefield. If those missions and objectives are not being met, either adjustments need to be made or new ones need to be established. A good military leader must always have a clear vision of what is to be accomplished and the right path to get there.

> *"Where there is no vision, the people perish: but he that keepeth the law, happy is he."*
> *Proverbs 29:18 KJV*

When a Commander is placed on a battlefield, he is assigned certain "Areas of Operation." These are referred to as an AO. His superiors assign him to a particular land mass in which he is given the tasks and responsibilities of protecting and securing. In war, that is his area of responsibility and he must take command of it.

Just like with military commanders, our King has given each of His Lionheart Warriors Areas of Operations (AOs) for which they are accountable. These AOs are our duty stations. They are our territories on this earth and it is our duty to take command of those areas. We have been tasked to provide, protect and secure all the King desires there.

In order to better understand the territories God has assigned us, we must see our lives in a new light. Our Areas of Operation are made up of three distinct, but interlocked regions; The Personal, The Relational and the Territorial. These three areas represent the warriors sphere of influence on this earth and we are given authority over them. They each represent the major sections in the warrior's life.

It can best be understood like so:

Personal — How we deal with ourselves, or internal world. The day to day, moment by moment interaction within your mind, body and spirit.

Relational — How we deal with our friends and family. Those relationships that make up the intimate connections in our lives. All interactions with other people in all their nuances, from those closest to us, to those we meet for the very first time.

Territorial — How we deal with our world. Our lasting mark on society. How our gifts, talents and influence is established from the smallest professional goal to the largest personal goal.

The three areas of operation; Personal, Relational and Territorial are best understood as three interlocking rings or circles. All three of these areas are different sized rings wrapped around one another, like a target. (see diagram 1.1)

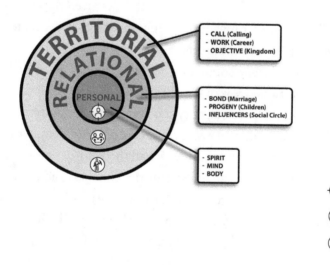

An inner ring, a middle ring and an outer ring. Three concentric rings expanding outward from a common center, each larger and farther away from the other.

The innermost ring represents those areas that are closest to the warrior. This area has the most ability to empower and affect the warrior, but it also will bring the most harm if not properly managed. The next ring, the middle, is connected to the first, but now takes on a less interpersonal role. This middle ring can be extremely empowering and harmful at the same time, but not as much as the first. As the rings move away from center, they are less under our influence and have the ability to draw the warrior off balance and over extended. The outermost ring is not necessarily of lesser importance than the first two, but its management requires more attention and support from the other areas and is most vulnerable to attack given its proximity to the center. Being farther away in influence, there is a lack of control. All areas in our lives are connected and therefore have impact on others. They each have major influence over us. Their influence has a residual effect, both good and bad.

Each of these three areas are broken down further into three component parts each. These component parts within each AO are known as battlefronts. Just like in war, battlefronts are the areas where there is enemy activity. The enemy has certain interests, agendas and strongholds. Ground is constantly gained and lost by them while pushing their agenda. These battlefronts are the real estate where offense and defense take place in conventional war. There are objectives and territory to capture by each party. On these fronts, the fighting can be intense and the casualties can be high. Battlefronts are the combat zones of war. They are where victories and defeats are had.

Just as in physical war, our battlefronts are places of fighting. These are the areas we Lionheart Warriors have a duty to protect and steward. Importantly, this is where we will take the fight to the enemy. In these AOs, the Lionheart Warrior will have ever evolving objectives, missions and tasks needing to be accomplished. A constant state of adaptation and improvisation are necessary. We are to be on guard and to know the status of our areas at all times. God has warned us that authority does not always last from one generation to another. A degrading effect must be acknowledged and be taken into account. We must be vigilant. Having been mandated by the King, the warrior has the responsibility to use his or her talents and gifts to protect, defend and conquer these areas in life.

At face value, these responsibilities can seem overwhelming. God has provided the will and means to accomplish all we will face for His Kingdom. In the end, it will come down to whether we use what has been provided or not. The temptation to "wing it" or be complacent is dangerous and must be avoided at all costs. The enemy is crafty, determined and hopes the warrior is weak and sleeping while on duty.

> *The King has hand-picked us for each of our specific areas in life.*

The King has hand-picked us for each of our specific areas in life. Each warrior was hand-selected based on the Lord's will and design. All this in order to maximize His glory in our areas. Knowing the strategy and plan, the enemy is going to come out against us in full bore. The fighting will exist on a spiritual plane, which may or may not manifest physically. Therefore, warfare is not fought like conventional warfare. We will not always see the enemy moving in on the horizon. The fighting may have physical or natural components, but for the most part is conducted in the heavenly realms. Since the source of the struggle is spiritual, our tools and tactics must be utilized accordingly.

> *"For we wrestle not against flesh and blood, but against principalities, against powers, against the rulers of the darkness of this world, against spiritual wickedness in high places."*
> *Ephesians 6:12 KJV*

Keep in mind, the enemy has honed their skills through all the centuries. By use of trial and error, they have practiced getting it right. We as warriors must act intentionally and methodically by relying on the tools and strength God has provided. We must look to Him as our source of power. The ability to uphold these duties is outside the warrior's natural abilities and we must trust and follow the instructions and guidance in the Lord's plan.

In order to develop the right and proper strategy, the warrior must thoroughly understand and be intimate with the weaknesses and strengths in their Areas of Operation. As we move forward in this study, we will breakdown the AOs down into further detail. We will try to understand our roles and responsibilities and why they are so vital to the overall mission. We will study God's provisions and power provided specifically for each area and how to implement them. We will understand why all this is important to accomplishing our missions and how to evolve as warriors for God's glory.

Be on guard, the enemy is at hand!

Chapter 7

Impenetrable Armor

"Therefore take up the whole armor of God, that you may be able to withstand in the evil day, and having done all, to stand. Stand therefore, having girded your waist with truth, having put on the breastplate of righteousness, and having shod your feet with the preparation of the gospel of peace; above all, taking the shield of faith with which you will be able to quench all the fiery darts of the wicked one. And take the helmet of salvation, and the sword of the Spirit, which is the word of God;"
Ephesians 6:13-17 NKJV

While working as a police officer in the Washington D.C. area, we started all our shifts with a meeting known as roll call. The roll call was a squad get together at the station where information, duty assignments and any announcements could be passed along to the unit. It also was an opportunity for a supervisor to make sure all their officers had all their issued gear, things such as uniform, body armor, duty belt, batons, radios, etc. The supervisors understood the importance of that gear and that it needed to be in good working order, so that their officers could properly do their job. Annually, we would undergo training to ensure we were proficient with all that issued equipment. Heaven forbid an officer got into an altercation and was unable to protect him- or herself due to lack of improper training with their gear.

Since officers go out into hostile environments, not only must they have the proper equipment, but they must know how to use it. Once the fight is already on, it will be too late to learn their proper use. As in all things, we will never rise to the occasion, but always fall to the level of our training. In the moment of battle, it all comes down to preparation.

Once we as Lionheart Warriors undergo a change of heart and receive the forgiveness provided by God, we are no longer at war with our Creator. In our new self, we no longer fight against His will and glory. Upon our decision to follow Christ, we vowed to never again raise arms against His crown. God put His Spirit within us and we no longer want to strive in rebellion. Since we switched sides, we now fight for the right team.

Bear in mind, having switched sides in the middle of an on-going war does not give us a free pass to stay out of the on-going fight. We simply just switched the direction of our fighting. Just because we vowed to no longer fight against God, doesn't mean we stopped fighting all together. We have been given a new perspective. We are still called to wage war, just not for the side we once did. We are now soldiers in God's Army. Fighting for His rule and authority and not our own. We now strive to push His agenda and not that of the enemy. Based on this new development in our life, the enemy will launch vicious attacks against us that were once meant for others.

Unfortunately, we do not fully realize the gravity of the war we are locked in. We do not fully grasp the determination of our enemy. We do not fully appreciate the lengths they will go to create discord and havoc in the life of the warrior. Basically, if the enemy can make God's warriors look weak and divided, they consider it a partial victory.

As part of the overall enemy strategy, they look to make the redeemed warriors of God ineffective before they can even get started. The enemy knows the power of a warrior "sold-out" for the Kingdom and will try and delay that as long as possible. This goal is easily accomplished if we do not know their schemes. As God's warriors, we need to be taking the fight back at them. We must be formidable in our pursuit. God's warriors need to be securing the areas He has given them. We must be methodical in our defenses against their onslaughts. We need to tear down their strongholds, which hold us at bay. We must be unrelenting in our assault on the enemy.

Since Almighty God has provided the warrior with all the tools and support necessary to engage in this fight, it is up to us to use them. It is up to us to master God's offensive and defensive weapons. Ultimately, we need to understand the tools He has given us and how to effectively bear them for His glory.

> *Our King's armor is spiritually designed and crafted in such a way to provide the Lionheart Warrior with all the protection needed to stand up against enemy assaults.*

As stated in the opening scripture in this chapter, we as warriors are given a set of armor. This is not just any set of armor, but God's armor. As you can imagine, the King's armor has to be the best. Even in human circles, the king's armor was the best a blacksmith could design. Let's face it, if a king in the past was injured, because there was a defect in the king's armor, that blacksmith was probably not making anymore armor. Our King's armor is spiritually designed and crafted in such a way to provide the Lionheart Warrior with all the protection needed to stand up against enemy assaults. His armor is perfect and vital. It is sufficient for every attack the enemy could possibly levy and must be relied upon in every single instance. We need to understand the fight before us and how it can only be won using the armor God has provided.

Being ever deceptive, the enemy will attempt to convince us the attack is not a severe enough of a threat to call on this armor. Our flesh will make it seem as though we can handle the assault under our own power and without using the tools God provides. Many of God's warriors have received unnecessary wounds by falling under this false belief.

Knowing that our arrogance and self sufficiency is one of our biggest problems, the enemy tempts us to go at it alone. We naturally think we can handle the little things and we do not need to bring them before the King. By our own power, we try and take care of things ourselves. Despite this temptation, we must not give in, but instead rely on God's provisions in our fight. Specifically the use of His armor. With no other way to find success, the enemy has no other choice but to try and separate the warrior from their armor.

God's armor consists of five pieces, all with a specific purpose and use. Each of these pieces are designed to be used practically as well as strategically. It is important to note that we will find much of the armor's effectiveness in the preparation for an impending attack. In effectively deploying the armor, we come to realize God is the one actually doing all the fighting. His armor keeps our minds focused and in the right perspective. As Lionheart Warriors, our power is in staying focused on Who it is doing the real fighting. Ultimately, it is all God's fight. This is God's war and in Him, victory has already been secured.

Since our victory is assured, we need this truth as a constant reminder. By understanding each piece of armor, we are provided a way to remind us that victory has already been achieved. The armor provides a daily reminder of His provisions for us. In the individual pieces, we recount how He obtained the victory through His Son on the cross. The armor is a beacon reminding us how Christ our King taught us to be humble. How He instructed us to deny ourselves daily. We, as His followers, are to die to self. We are to die to our abilities and to whatever strength we think we may possess. We are to die to our ego and all the self-glorification it represents. We are to let go and truly be free. Daily, we must remember just how we came to be in our place of victory. How we even came to know about this war at all.

Only through going before Christ's cross, humbling ourselves and trusting in His grace, are we able to operate. By putting on this mindset, we are ready to enter the armor room and begin to put on God's armor. It is a reminder that the good news of our redemption by Jesus is the only way to power. Otherwise, putting on some sort of holy armor is just a nice thing to think about while making ourselves feel more spiritual.

Each piece of God's armor reveals the power to fight the enemy by what Jesus did on the cross. By examining each piece individually, we get a better understanding of God's path to victory. As we work from the head down to the feet, let us breakdown each piece of His armor in detail.

THE HELMET OF SALVATION:

One of the most vulnerable areas of the human body in combat is the head. Heads are home to our brains. Since the mind is responsible for all our decision making abilities, it is important we protect it in combat. Why would God designate the piece of armor responsible for protecting the mind, "salvation?" Why not designate the helmet of "peace" instead? If we are making the connection between thoughts and how they relate to spiritual warfare, then why not a piece of armor which aides in thinking peaceful thoughts?

Let's face it, feelings of peace are very attractive from a worldly perspective. If given an opportunity to provide advice on dealing with attacks on the mind, the world would definitely advise us to think good, happy thoughts. They would recommend we be optimistic and just stay positive, right? Why would God choose "salvation" as the protective element for the mind, instead of something else more applicable?

I want you to take a moment and imagine you are an athlete in a competitive sport such as football. What if I told you ahead of time, no matter what happens during your upcoming game, your team is going to be victorious. No matter what happens during the game, your side wins. You will be the victor and will receive all the accolades associated with winning the game. Your end result will be victory, no matter what actually happened during the game. You will be declared champion and there is nothing you can do to undermine it.

How would that truth affect your performance while actually playing that game? Would it make a difference in your decision making process? Would you find yourself being more careful or would you play with more boldness? Would you be more conservative in your play selection or do you think you would take more chances? Do you think you would get easily disappointed at setbacks and hardships or do you think you would just quickly brush them off?

Remember, victory is a done deal; you know you will win the game no matter what. You are absolutely convinced based on rock-solid information that you cannot lose. Let us say you had supernatural abilities to see the results and nothing could change those results. There will be no alternate outcomes. You are the winner. Failure is an impossibility, because your victory is assured.

That is salvation!

This truth changes everything. It puts all the highs and lows of life in their right perspectives. It creates in you a hope and a belief that's utterly contagious. Despite the circumstances, salvation creates a confidence that radiates your entire demeanor. Your mentality is one of complete and total victory. A mind wrapped securely in thoughts of complete and utter victory, just like a helmet.

Helmets are a defensive covering that protects the head of a warrior and all the thoughts that flow in and out of it. Take for instance the senses — sight, sound, smell, touch, taste. They are how our bodies receive information from the physical world. They obviously play a crucial role in our total sense of self and reality. What comes our way through these senses are processed by the mind and therefore effect how we interact in life.

These sensations of self are how the enemy will confront us. There is a spiritual component to the physical realities of our world. It knows we battle a fleshly enemy nature from within and that nature's ultimate motivation is self-preservation. Our fallen nature uses everything in its environment to serve its own ends. This negative desire is the root of fear.

Fear is born from a sense of insecurity. Insecurity from a lack of control. Ultimate lack of control is revealed in the fact of our inevitable death. Death is unavoidable and the fleshly nature in us is haunted by it. The ultimate fear of failure and loss. The fear of death is the chief of all fears, because it is the cliff of existence. It is the end of the road for the flesh. It is the clock when it hits zero. All fears are born from here. Failure and loss at all levels find their realization in death. The enemy uses this fear to manipulate. It hangs this timetable and destiny in front of the warrior's flesh to cause doubt and powerlessness. It knows succumbing to fear will lead the warrior to falter in the fight and give them a foot hold.

God's gift of salvation needs to permeate all areas of our thinking. If the enemy tries to sow seeds of doubt in our mind, it must be filtered through our sense of self as it pertains to God's plan of salvation. It must consist of our understanding of who we are and what we are about in Christ. A fixed understanding of our true destiny and destination. The enemy will try and convince us of our inadequacies and in doing so, hamper our cause. Therefore, it is his way of ambushing any action we may take for God's kingdom.

Salvation is the antidote to this fear. If we are convinced that no matter what happens we will be rescued and saved, there is nothing we will not attempt to do for our King. Spiritual boldness springs forth from this understanding.

Let's go back to our sports analogy again. If you knew that, no matter what, you would come out on the other end of a competition as victorious, is there any contest or game you would be to afraid to enter?

The ultimate fear being death, salvation cancels that out. If the consequences of death are alleviated, then ultimately, there is nothing to fear on this side of it. Death is but a doorway into salvation for the believer. This fact compels courage; a courage to go forth and conquer despite the perceived risks. Since the enemy cannot attack our abilities to perform, it will go after us more personally. Since it cannot cause us to doubt what we can do, it will try to attack who we are. It will go after our sense of self and how we measure up.

THE BREASTPLATE OF RIGHTEOUSNESS:

The breastplate was a hardened garment that protected the vital organs of the warrior. It covered the chest and abdomen from attack on the body. It shielded the center mass. This proactive layer protects the heart and lungs. It blocks slashes and thrusts from the enemy to the core. It provides an unshakeable confidence at the center. God's breastplate of righteousness has a similar function.

Through the redemptive work of the Son of God, the Lionheart Warrior has been given absolute righteousness. We are given Christ's own personal righteousness as our own. The warrior is made morally perfect. We are declared pure and undefiled. We are at right standing before God. All our past transgressions and imperfections are abolished. We are untouchable from the guilt and shame associated with past sins. God performed a cosmic swap on the cross. Christ's righteousness became ours and our sin became His. We were given new standing before God regardless of our feelings. Our shame of past failures were declared to be unfounded and useless going forward. These facts infuriate our enemy.

The enemy will try and attack the warrior from the place we used to be. It will remind us of our past indiscretions and failures. The enemy will try to remind us of where we came from. It will attempt to use past information to guilt, shame and condemn the warrior to a life of inaction and hesitancy in doing the right thing.

Learning to utilize God's breastplate of righteousness will thwart these attempts by the enemy before they even start. Our understanding of Christ's gift of righteousness and its ramifications make these attacks ineffective. In these areas, the enemy's use of regret and shame are ineffective against the warrior. We are no longer that way. Our core being is covered by righteousness and therefore impervious to this type of assault.

Using the same competition analogy from before, imagine that no matter how this game went down, you would come out on the other end looking like the hero. Despite your performance either way, you will be considered the most valuable player. You will be seen by all involved as the star performer. The best of the best.

We have Christ's righteousness and are viewed as Him, not us. He is perfect and that perfection is transferred to us. The record will show a flawless performance on our behalf, despite what has been accomplished in our past or even will be accomplished in our future. Imagine no one will ever see it any other way. You are declared righteous, perfect, and flawless. You can never go wrong or be seen as having done wrong, because God has declared that your performance reflects that of His Son and not your own.

How would that affect your sense of self-worth or shame? How would this affect your fears of failure going forward? You can never be accused of screwing up. You can never be found lacking or wanting. You will always exceed all expectations and performance criteria under fire. Will it free you up to give your all without the fear of failure? Should that fear of failure ever really hold you back from your purpose?

What an amazing gift.

What an amazing truth.

THE BELT OF TRUTH:

From the very beginning, the enemy brought mankind into this war by attacking truth. It questioned the reality of God's truth in the mind of man. It sowed seeds of doubt and alternate truths to humans and they fell for it. They choose the false truth over God's truth. The enemy is the father of lies and uses it as his primary weapon of warfare. The best weapon to fight lies is truth. Not any truth, but God's truth.

The warrior is equipped with this centerpiece to the armor in which all the other pieces hang, God's belt of truth. The warrior relies on the truth to be the centerpiece of the defense against the enemy. We are convinced of the truth revealed to us and the truth of our purpose and mission. This truth strengthens and re-enforces the center of who we are and what we are doing in this war.

We go back to this centerpiece of truth whenever we are under assault from the lies of the enemy. By tying all the armor together, this truth is what holds the warrior up and combats all the lies. What exactly is this truth? The truth of who God is and what He has done, is doing and will do for us in this war. The warrior hangs on this. The warrior trusts in this and this truth makes us secure.

God's belt (also referred to as Girdle of Truth) provides a glue to the armor. It is the centerpiece. It helps us understand the concept of girding up. A girdle is designed to tighten in and strap down a person's intestines and pelvic region. Our core and sense of equilibrium. Our stomach region is our soft spot. It's our exposed belly and genital region. Our ultimate physical weakness.

Drawing in one's belt brings things tighter to the center, thus providing confidence and stability. As a warrior will tell you when engaged in any physical contact situation, the mind naturally goes to protecting two primary places, the head and our pelvic region. It's an automatic response. An armored girdle relieves us of that concern of a low blow. It acts as a protective jock strap. It keeps them close and secure, giving us physical confidence and insuring we can give our absolute all in the engagement.

This hip area is the center of a warrior's balance and the point at which we will ultimately bare any force applied in combat. Every athlete knows the power resides in the hips; the seat of true physical power. Truth provides this to us in the same way. Truth does not leave the warrior naked, weak and exposed to being dominated by the enemy. With it, we can have utter confidence in our intentions, actions, mission and protection.

God's truth provides this to the warrior. It is the foundation of understanding toward the other pieces of God's armor. Truth provides the seat of power from which the other pieces draw their meaning and strength. It is the foundation of God's movement in the warrior's life. Truth grabs the warrior at the core.

THE SANDALS OF PEACE:

To understand the role the sandals play, we must appreciate the role of walking. Footwear carries us where we want to go in life's journey. They protect our feet and give us sure footing in unstable terrain. The warrior's footwear must provide all this and more. We will be under hostile conditions, so therefore our footwear must be suited for the environment in which we operate.

Sandals carry the warrior to the destination and provide the ability to keep moving forward or stand on firm ground while under attack. The sandals are important in giving the Lionheart Warrior purpose in our calling and emphasizing the importance of our mission and movement in right directions. The Gospel of peace the Son bought on the cross, fuels the warrior's purpose and defines the mission. We rely on this message to give us our ultimate marching orders. Understanding the gospel of Christ is how God has chosen to expand His glory and Kingdom. The Gospel provides us with His targeted cause and ultimate direction of our travel.

> *"How beautiful upon the mountains Are the feet of him*
> *who brings good news, Who proclaims peace, Who brings*
> *glad tidings of good things, Who proclaims salvation,*
> *Who says to Zion, "Your God reigns!" -Isaiah 52:7 NKJV*

While studying the armor of God, I often struggled with how sandals acted as pieces of armor. What exactly do they protect? Why would the Holy Spirit through the Apostle Paul want the Lionheart Warrior to know about armored footwear?

It seemed to me at the time as though Paul ran out of pieces of armor and just threw this one out there. Let's be honest, if you have ever heard someone speak on the armor of God, they either do not mention the sandals or do not go into much detail concerning them. This piece of armor is not the one (along with the girdle) put on t-shirts and bumper stickers. This one does not invoke thoughts of *Braveheart* or *Gladiator* in people's minds. It lacks cool points and is mostly skipped over for lack of inspiration. What a grave mistake this is and totally misses out on the their protection and power.

Imagine you are in a situation where no matter what you do, you will accomplish your desired goal. Imagine that every move you make, every action you attempt, gets you one step closer to your desired outcome. Keep in mind, some actions get you there faster than others, but in the end, you are going to ultimately be successful.

This concept is the sandals of peace. God has chosen to accomplish His glory in this way, by spreading the Gospel of peace to the lost. He chose us to conquer His enemies. The Lord's path to victory is through His Gospel and the peace it brings to His Kingdom. These sandals carry the warrior there. The sandals propel our every step toward God's glorious victory—glorious victory through spreading the good news of Christ's redeeming work.

THE SHIELD OF FAITH:

Every warrior needs a shield. Every warrior needs an object to hide behind when the attacks from the enemy become overwhelming. We know the enemy is going to launch all kind of attacks at us. In scripture, these attacks are described as fiery darts. Flaming hot and extremely dangerous darts meant not only to harm us, but engulf us in flames. These attacks are meant to disable and consume us.

With attacks like these, we need a formidable shield to protect not only our being, but all our individual pieces of armor. This shield needs to be mighty enough that it will re-enforce and protect all our armor. A shield of faith.

Faith is the expression and reliance on the truths outlined in scripture. Belief in the truth of God. A trusting belief in the plans and purposes of God. Faith that can be stood behind and relied upon for protection and strength while under the worst kinds of attack.

In God's armor, the shield is the only primarily defensive piece of armor not physically attached to the warrior. Since it is not fixed on the person, it can be moved and positioned in different ways to repel enemy attacks as needed. Shields come in all shapes and sizes. Smaller ones for mobility and ease of carry and larger ones to protect the warrior from head to toe. We are told that varying levels of faith are given to the warrior. The shield of faith is used in conjunction with all other pieces and ensures the complete protection of the warrior while under threat.

THE SWORD OF THE SPIRIT (WORD OF GOD)

By design, swords are both an offensive and a defensive weapon. They can deliver critical blows to the enemy in the form of slashes and stabs. The sword can be used to block enemy attacks, as well as divert them off their intended target with a parry.

God's word works exactly in this manner. It has the power to defeat any of God's enemies in an instant. His word is always effective, despite us seeing the final results of its blow. Jesus demonstrated the effectiveness of God's word by relying exclusively upon it while under assault by Satan in the desert. In His earthly mission, the Son was lead into the desert to face the angel of darkness head on. While being attacked by the dark one, He remained vigilant and simply quoted God's word to the Devil every time an attack was made. By effectively doing this, it caused the Devil to retreat.

In order to be effective, the Sword of the Spirit must be unsheathed and deployed. God's word spoken over circumstances and especially in prayer goes forth to accomplish His will. The warrior must be constantly involved in saturating their mind with the Word of God. By doing this, the Holy Spirit will wield the sword in their time of need.

In order to get stronger and be effective fighters, the scriptures tell us that we are to constantly be searching and studying His word. We need to have a good command of the sword in battle. We need to train with it extensively to become more proficient at its deployment. Like the shield of faith, the sword is to be used in conjunction with the other pieces of armor, creating a complete and total warrior. God's word is powerful and accomplishes exactly what He intends for it to accomplish. We as warriors are simply to utilize it in battle.

As we can see, Almighty God has given us an incredibly powerful set of tools to fight against the enemy. We as Lionheart Warriors are fully equipped and provided for when the attacks come our way. We have a duty to understand all His armor's capabilities and to how to deploy them with precision, for our enemy is formidable and scouring the earth looking for a fight.

Time to strap on and strap in, for the fight is on!

CHAPTER 8
BATTLEFIELD COMMUNICATIONS

While in the Marine Corps, I worked as a sentry guarding different military installations. Often times, I stood guard at one of the entry points to that installation, referred to as a gate. At the time, gate duty was divided into six-hour shifts. While on post, we were required to conduct radio checks with our dispatch back at the guard shack. A radio check was an equipment check where we attempt to communicate via our issued handheld radio at predetermined times. These radio checks provided the guard force with two basic things: 1) It made sure the radios were functioning properly by transmitting in both directions adequately. Basically, the guard could hear the dispatch and the dispatch could hear the guard, loud and clear. 2) The radio check also provided a welfare check to the Marine on post. This welfare check gave opportunity at designated times for some sort of communication to take place. In case the Marine was having any issues or may need assistance, the radio check opened up that channel of communication with on duty superiors. On the battlefield, clear lines of communications are a vital component to military success. A radio check's intended goal was to establish "Good Comms," or good communication.

With new advancements in technology, the battlefield has become a very fluid environment for commanders to direct their troops quickly in a fight. On ancient battlefields, communication was slow or even nonexistent for leaders to make adjustments to their troops mission and movements. Due to lack of communication in major battles, superior forces could suffer sever losses to substantially inferior forces.

Given the stakes are very high in battle, military commanders must have the ability to issue orders and receive feedback in an instant. Especially in hostile environments, their new orders need to be carried out at a moment's notice. Commanders must have up-to-date intelligence of what is transpiring and the battle's current conditions. While engaged in combat, failure to communicate with a leader is unacceptable and will lead to catastrophic failure to the mission and personnel. The same holds true for our spiritual battlefield.

As we learned previously, God has placed His Spirit within us. He did this so we can be in constant fellowship and communication with Him. In doing this, He gave us the ability to rely on His promptings and directions in all our situations. Our connection through the Spirit allows us to receive His guidance and direction. As a concept, this is very simple to understand, but very difficult to apply, due to our incompetence. God provides us with two basic tools for communication, one for communicating with Him and the other for Him to communicate with us. Unfortunately, at times our side of communication gets blocked, because we carry "poor reception."

God provides us with two basic tools for communication, one for communicating with Him and the other for Him to communicate with us.

As mentioned previously about our fallenness, we have hardwiring from our old nature that gets in the way. That old nature crosses up our wires by sending and receiving false orders and directions. This is a constant reality and we cannot fully escape it this side of eternity. In His provision, God provided ways for us to deal with this old undermining nature. Our King desires to give us clear direction and guidance. He provides a way to differentiate between His comms and those of our old fleshly nature.

LISTENING TO GOD SPEAK

Throughout human history, God has always communicated with His people by speaking to key individuals at key times. Each time He spoke to them, more and more of His truth was revealed to the world. All these truths were written down and compiled through the centuries. The writings were passed down and held very sacred. They were duplicated and transferred with delicate precision in order to preserve their divine message to mankind.

In the last days, God revealed His truth through His Son, Jesus. The Son confirmed the truths God revealed previously and empowered His followers to carry on the spreading of that truth to the world. These writings were compiled and placed into what we currently refer to as the *Holy Bible*.

> *"All Scripture is given by inspiration of God, and is profitable for doctrine, for reproof, for correction, for instruction in righteousness, that the man of God may be complete, thoroughly equipped for every good work."*
> *II Timothy 3:16-17 NKJV*

It is through reading and studying these Holy writings by His Spirit that we can understand the will of God for His Kingdom. Through His Word, He has provided sufficient instruction for all things necessary to our mission. The Lionheart Warrior has utmost confidence that the promptings received from diligent study of the Word are from God.

In desiring to follow the King aright, we must take the totality of His scripture into account. Through the power of the Spirit He placed inside us, the warrior will be guided into all His truth. Essential to fighting this war is the discipline of going to the Word and trusting that God will speak through it. This is how the King has designated His instruction will be given to His warriors. Through the teachings of His word, He makes adjustments in our lives. This is how we develop and get stronger in might. God's power for the warrior is in His spoken word.

Through diligent study of the truth of God's word, the Lionheart Warrior can lash out at the enemy. Previously we learned about the power of the sword. The Word of God is mighty to cut deep at the heart of the enemy and deep into our own souls. There is no other way. We are tasked to study and show ourselves approved to Him through studying it deeply and by only His word are we truly fed.

GOD IS LISTENING

Now knowing the Lord's way to receive instruction is through His word, the communication does not stop there. It is not a one-way street. He wants us to communicate with Him as well. He desires we share all our struggles, cares, wants and needs in real time. He wants to hear our opinions on things. God designed us to be in fellowship with Him. The desire for this fellowship is built into our very being. The desire to talk with Him is inherent within us. It is in our spiritual DNA. We communicate with Him to function spiritually. Speaking with God is specifically designed to refresh our souls.

Despite His omniscience, God wants to hear our perspective and for us to express how we feel our fight is going. He uses our interactions with Him in ways that go well beyond the current situation. He uses it in ways we cannot fully comprehend on a natural level. The more we communicate with Him, the stronger our bond with Him becomes and we grow as His warriors. This form of communication is referred to as prayer.

Prayer is nothing more than a spiritual conversation, where we speak directly to the King. The beauty is at any and all times, we can express our thoughts and concerns to the Lord of all. Depending on our desires and needs, the extent and duration of the communiqués can vary. As far as level of importance, the King has revealed to us through His word that nothing is too small or insignificant for Him to be briefed about.

Since God already knows the request ahead of time, our prayers can even be rather short in nature.

Christ taught us that we should never try and impress Him in prayer. God is not impressed with our many fancy or formal words. We are to simply speak our hearts in trust, believing that we are being heard. To put it simply, we need to get to the point and just pour out our hearts while holding nothing back. We will find that mighty power is had in being able to address our Commander anytime we desire. We are commanded to pray at all times and in all circumstances.

Since our communication with the King is both mandated and necessary for spiritual life, we need an idea about how to go about accomplishing it. Is there a prescribed way laid out in His word? Are there specific instructions on what prayer must look like? The short answer is both a yes and a no. When Jesus' followers asked Him how they should pray, He taught them a short model prayer. It (known as The Lord's Prayer) acts as a formula for approaching God and is as follows:

> "Our Father who art in heaven
> Hollowed be Thy Name
> Thy Kingdom Come, Thy will be done on earth as it
> is in heaven
> Give us this day our daily bread
> Forgive us our trespasses, as we forgive those who trespass
> against us
> Lead us not into temptation, but deliver us from evil
> For Thine is the Kingdom and the power and the glory,
> forever and ever."

Being the most memorized prayer in history, it is important to understand that this prayer is not a magic spell or supernatural incantation. It is simply a model for communication with God. We know this because Jesus commanded His followers to *pray like this*, as opposed to *pray this*.

Let's take a look at the individual lines of The Lord's Prayer and we will see His formula unfold.

First line, *"Our Father who art in Heaven,"* sets the tone for our relationship with God. God is to be viewed and addressed as our Divine Father, above and beyond our existence and reality. This is a sign of intimacy and familiarity. It goes beyond master and servant, creator and creature. There is a loving bond and connection unique to a child.

He is a King who is loving.

"Hollowed be Thy Name" Here we see His position. We are to keep Him as Lord God in the forefront of our minds. Even though the first line speaks of familiarity, the second line sets the tone for His place of reverence. He is almighty, holy and above all things. He is separated in status beyond our finite natural understanding. The line is an acknowledgment and appreciation for who He is in His essence.

He is a King who is holy.

"Thy Kingdom Come, Thy will be done on earth as it is in heaven." Here we see His agenda is priority and utmost in our minds. We acknowledge and pledge our loyalty to His cause and desire the things which He desires. We recognize His absolute sovereignty both in heaven and on earth.

He is a King who is sovereign.

"Give us this day our daily bread." This line speaks to our acknowledgement that all good things come from Him. We ask for every necessary provision in our day. This line speaks of prayer being an everyday occurrence. The line implies that we should not go a day without being reliant on Him for all our needs.

He is a King who is gracious.

"Forgive us our trespasses, as we forgive those who trespass against us." This line sets the standard for our dealings with our fellow man. In the line, we ask for forgiveness from the Lord with a specific condition. We are only asking to be forgiven in the same way we forgive others. Often overlooked or misunderstood, this line is to be a constant reminder we are to forgive as much as we are forgiven. This speaks to the Lord's desire for reconciliation and fellowship amongst His people. He wants cohesion in the Kingdom in all areas, especially Kingdom relationships.

He is a King who is forgiving.

"Lead us not into temptation, but deliver us from evil." This line reminds us we are to follow the King's promptings, plans and directions in all our daily dealings. We are to follow His wise leading and not the world's or our former debased desires. We acknowledge His leadership and request we be spared a path that will put us at risk for rebelling against Him.

In addition, this line speaks to our reliance on our relationship with Him and the fact that we do not want it disrupted. We are therefore willing servants not wanting anything to come between us and our King. The line also recognizes the Lord is the one who will rescue us and protect us from evil. We acknowledge our lack of skill and power to deliver us from said evil and therefore must trust in Him.

He is a King who is protector

"For Thine is the Kingdom and the power and the glory, forever and ever." This last line closes out the communication with an acknowledgment and recognition of the King's ultimate authority and power over all things. It shows all He possesses. He owns the Kingdom. He owns all the power and He owns all the glory. Not only does He own it, He owns

it forever without end. This line is a direct assault toward any entity who rebels against God. This is a line of allegiance to the Most High. The line is an acknowledgement of His ultimate authority in all things.

He is a King who is supreme

Communication is vital. God has given us warriors mighty tools to accomplish our mission. Through the daily disciplines of *Bible* study and prayer, the Lionheart Warrior will be equipped to take on the objectives God has laid before us and thwart the attacks of the enemy as they occur.

Understand a major component to the enemy's fight is to try and prevent us from relying upon God's communication tools. The enemy is fully aware the power a warrior has when these tools are mastered. The enemy understands the lethality we have when we are rooted in communication with our King.

Let us be diligent to remain in His presence.

SECTION III
INNER RING

CHAPTER 9
HEAD QUARTERS

Years ago, the U.S. Army had a recruiting campaign with the tagline "Army of One." By trying to entice the individual to invest in themselves, the Army had hoped to gain a fresh new crop of recruits wanting to become soldiers. Prior to the "Army of One" marketing campaign, they used the slogan, "Be All You Can Be." Both these slogans shared a commonality, they called out the individual by encouraging them to take next steps toward making themselves something better.

Let's face it, the individual soldier is the key component to winning any battle in war. Boots on the ground secure territory and securing territory is victory. The individual soldier must be useful, loyal and proficient to this end. If individual soldiers are undertrained, lack military discipline and cannot perform their duties effectively, then the larger unit will suffer—potentially the entire military campaign and all its objectives.

Having effective soldiers is essential to victory. If you spread one individual soldier's problem out over the entire unit, you will have a damaging effect on the mission capability and therefore potentially alter the effectiveness of the entire unit. Basically, the problem does not stay with just the one soldier. There is a chain effect that compounds over that military force. Imagine this inadequacy was the standard of proficiency for the entire army. The results would be catastrophic. If that lack of competency were the minimum standard, then all would eventually be lost before the first shots were ever fired in combat.

In the military, warriors are given a certain level of basic training. They develop a general skillset as a foundation. A certain amount of information and skill is invested to build up them up in order to accomplish a particular job in the fight. By implementing this standard of skill across the mass of warriors, you will get a proficient unit working in sync with one another. Multiply those units and you have a mighty army. With the right army, you can accomplish any military mission set before you.

Just as in conventional armies, the same logic holds true in God's Kingdom. Training starts at the individual Lionheart Warrior level. We must first understand what makes us tick. We, as newly converted Lionheart Warriors, are composed of three basic parts at our core: spirit, mind and body. These parts work in conjunction.

This is a new development in the warrior. If you remember, prior to our rescue and redemption, we were dead in our spirit. We practically did not have one. At that time, we were under the direct control of the fleshly fallen nature and hopelessly susceptible to the influences of the greater enemy. This manifested itself in either direct or indirect rebellion against our Creator. Once rescued and redeemed by the King, we were given His spirit and made a new creation in Christ. Only after this regeneration can we receive the things of God and follow His directions for our life. Only now can we get our headquarters under control and working for the King. The mind is now free to think after the things of God and get the body to follow suit.

The mind is the seat of our thoughts, will, likes, dislikes and sense of self. Our personality is found there and is an accumulation of all our experiences, knowledge and understanding of our world. This area was left to its own devices prior to the rescue and operated out of selfish interest. Some individuals were more self-interested than others, but in the end, we all served our own fallen nature to one extent or another. As a new creation, the warrior has a mind receptive to the promptings of His Spirit and develops new desires and behaviors.

The body is obviously the vehicle in which we carry out day-to-day operations our mind conceives. Our bodies come in varying shapes, colors and sizes. The body has grown as it moved from childhood to adulthood. As the warrior gets older, the body is going to degenerate and breakdown more and more due to age and disease. This can be slowed to a certain extent, but eventually the body will succumb to death and decay.

The body signals the mind by physical promptings which can either be beneficial or detrimental to the overall warrior. The body we live in has a direct influence on our mental and emotional state. There is a super connection between the two. It communicates through impulses to request and sometimes even demand certain things. Our conscious mind controls some of the body's functions and some of the functions it does not. The body is one of the biggest influencers over the mind and needs to be recognized as such. Pleasure and pain are extremely powerful motivators for the mind and most come from impulses driven by the body.

The spirit, mind and body make up the first battlefront in which the Lionheart Warrior will wage war. They are our headquarters and inner ring. We have been tasked by our King to fight inside this personal area on a daily basis. This will be a constant battle day in day out until the day our physical body succumbs to death. Some days the fight will be easier than others. Waging this war requires discipline, perseverance and understanding. The rest of our areas will depend on how well we operate here. The results of the spirit, mind and body battlefronts will filter over into our middle and outer rings.

In the three chapters that follow, we will look at each of these battlefronts in our inner ring AO (Area of Operation) individually and get a good understanding of how to strengthen and defend them. Careful contemplation and study in this area will prove vital for winning our battles there. Like in a conventional army, time and effort must be invested in the individual soldier's development to be effective on the battlefield. If our headquarters is weak or compromised, an avalanche effect will take place and those other outer rings will be impossible to strengthen and defend. In conclusion, our fight begins within us and careful attention must be taken to understand and master its parts. Moving forward, let's take a look at these critical sections of our first area of operation, the inner ring.

CHAPTER 10
THE FIGHTING SPIRIT

"However, when He, the Spirit of truth, has come, He will guide you into all truth; for He will not speak on His own authority, but whatever He hears He will speak; and He will tell you things to come."
John 16:13 NKJV

After graduating the Prince Georges County Police Academy, I was assigned to a squad and placed under the supervision and guidance of a Field Training Officer (FTO). The FTO's job was to provide me with on the job training. He acted as a mentor and advisor which assisted me in learning to apply all the training I had received at the police academy. During my FTO phase, at no time was I apart from him. We were basically joined at the hip. Since the job of police officer was so dangerous, part of his role as FTO was to constantly bring my attention to potential mistakes and scenarios that could get me or someone else seriously hurt. Always with my safety in mind, my FTO constantly provided critical direction and feedback to improve my on the job performance. While in the FTO period of training, I truly appreciated having an experienced mentor watching my back and leading me towards success and away from danger.

"Do you not know that you are the temple of God and that the Spirit of God dwells in you?"
I Corinthians 3:16 NKJV

In the moment where we as warriors decided to turn from our rebellion and received the pardon from Jesus Christ, a New Spirit was born within us. A new creation was formed inside of us. We received our own "FTO". Almighty God deposited His Spirit into the heart of the newly formed Lionheart Warrior. He gave Himself to dwell in our spirit. We were given 24/7 access and connected to Him at our deepest level. Being our personal advocate, this deposit was not a passive one, but one of power and action.

The Spirit of Power that raised Jesus from the dead now resides in the warrior. We have access to constant fellowship with Him. He becomes a part of us and our constant companion. As previously discussed, we have unfettered access all the time to His ear (prayer) and wisdom (word). Access to all the fullness of God and all the grace He provides. Our spiritual account is maxed out and we only need receive it through faith. The trusting reliance on His Spirit to guide us into the will and ways of our King. A placing of faith on Him and His work in and through us. Faith that is reality changing as it is acted upon. This faith will produce actionable steps. The warrior is a different person. Flowing from the inside out, we are different than before in our talking, walking and living. The change is a tangible manifestation of our new being.

> *Flowing from the inside out, we are different than before in our talking, walking and living.*

> "Therefore, if anyone is in Christ, he is a new creation; old things have passed away; behold, all things have become new."
> II Corinthians 5:17 NKJV

In our discussion of the fall, we learned before conversion the warrior's spirit was dead. Our spirit was lifeless. Our spirit was the equivalent of a rotting corpse. There was not a hint of life as it concerns fellowship with God's Spirit. Our state was DOA (dead on arrival). I know this fact can still be hard to swallow. At first hearing of it, our egos have a hard time accepting it. We want to believe we were good deep down. We want to believe we were just misunderstood. We were just spiritually sick, but not actually dead. Definitely not a rotting corpse. God's word is pretty cut and dry about our former state. Dead!

> *"And you He made alive, who were dead in trespasses*
> *and sins,"*
> *Ephesians 2:1 NKJV*

The state we were in caused us to seek our own way. We were lost. We chose selfishness instead of selflessness. We chose greed instead of giving. We chose pleasure instead of discipline. We chose arrogance instead of humility. We worked for ourselves longing to satisfy a need to prove we had worth. To prove we were something. To prove we were not all the things we actually were deep down. In our zeal for acceptance and satisfaction, we revealed our insecurity. We demonstrated our fear of the truth. The truth that we were inadequate. We were found lacking and we hated that. How dare you say, I'm inadequate. Who do you think you are talking to? Do you know who I am? Do you know what I have done? These are the ravings of scared little children hiding in the bushes, because they are naked and exposed.

We cover up. We manipulate. We hide and scheme to conceal the truth of who we really are, because we believe if its brought to light, we will be rejected. I know what you may be thinking at this point. Haven't we already gone over this? Do we really need to bring all of this back up?

Understanding our prior state is vital for two important reasons; 1) to comprehend the gracious gift of redemption offered to us through the Son. 2) In order to understand the remnants of the battles we will face in the future. Battles within ourselves. If we do not have a clear understanding of these things, it can lead to our spiritual complacency.

When a person goes to the doctor and is given hard news that he is gravely ill. He needs to believe the doctor and do what ever it is the doctor advises. That is if the patient wants to become healthy. He needs to understand the ailment, its symptoms and what it is the doctor wants him to do. If he doesn't believe the grave state of his condition, he will not take the steps necessary to combat the illness.

Thanks be to God in His mercy and grace, He did not leave the warrior in that former state. He did not leave us naked, afraid and in the bushes still plotting away. He redeemed us. He saved us. He rescued us from the pit of our despair. Upon receiving the provision through faith, He placed within us a new heart. He deposited within us His very own Spirit. He reversed the past and gave us a new life. With new power. With real confidence. Not the false confidence built on sand like before, but built on solid rock.

In depositing this Spirit, a change occurred. The warrior now has a righteousness of purpose which brings a lion to the forefront. A lion for Truth. A lion for God's Glory, not that shallow glory of the former self. This Lion resides in our Heart. It stands ready to fuel all our goings and comings. It drives us forward in a direction of meaning and purpose.

It is vital once this deposit occurs, for the warrior to rely on and look to the Spirit for direction. We as Lionheart Warriors need to be sensitive to His promptings and leadings. The Spirit is always present and desires to guide and lead us into the directions of God's plan. This is important, because the war still rages on. A war that now takes on a new front within us. A new battle waged within our being and our life. The Spirit is always vying for the warrior to follow His lead, but the other battlefronts of life are going to interfere.

Ever since the warrior came to terms with the rebellion by switching sides, the old ally (the enemy) has launched non-stop attacks. The enemy having lost the warrior to the King, will now mount attacks like never before. These attacks will divert attention away from the path of the Spirit. Through distraction and playing into the desires of our old fallen nature, we can be sidelined and sent back to our old rebellious ways. We will struggle to yield. We will resist the Spirit wanting to lead us. This is the first fight.

Being in constant battle to follow the Spirit and not the old nature, our flesh of self aggrandizement will constantly be looking for any and all opportunities to shut out our communication with the Spirit in our life. It is important from the very beginning to understand this struggle as a spiritual one and not as a physical one. A struggle requiring the tools provided to us by our Warrior King.

"For we wrestle not against flesh and blood, but against principalities, against powers, against the rulers of the darkness of this world, against spiritual wickedness in high places."
Ephesians 6:12 KJV

Lionheart Warriors have many weapons at their disposal when fighting this first phase of combat. Weapons like the Armor of God applied through prayer. As we have discussed earlier, the Lionheart King has provided us with these mighty weapons for battle. In this way, He is fighting for us. The Armor of God is not just some cute analogy to be inspired by, but actual weapons for war. All the armor must be consciously put on each and every day. Bear in mind, the Belt of Truth, the Breastplate of Righteousness and the Sandals of Peace are permanent and constant attire. They are to be worn at all times, never to be taken off. They provide our baseline status in Christ. Our Foundation of Understanding (Truth), our status as Warriors (Righteousness) and our Mission (Gospel of Peace) in the Kingdom. These three pieces are the keys to our identity in Christ. The three remaining pieces of the Salvation Helmet, Faith Shield and Word Sword are deployed when needed. These are always at our disposal and must be brought in to the fight whenever the enemy attacks.

Always remember, the armor is essential to winning our battles no matter how small or seemingly insignificant the fighting may seem. The conflict cannot be won without them. We have been given the Lord's strength and He has provided all we need. In order to access His provision, we must only ask and the grace is ours.

Be assured, the enemy is going to try and knock us back. It is going to try and knock us down. The warrior is to use all of God's provisions available to stand the ground. To stand firm in the place He put us. We are to stand firm and take charge of the Areas of Operation He has assigned to us. Reliance upon the Spirit is the first battlefront won for His Kingdom.

This is our duty and this is the Fight!

CHAPTER 11
THE COMBAT MIND

*"And do not be conformed to this world, but be transformed
by the renewing of your mind, that you may prove what is
that good and acceptable and perfect will of God."*
Romans 12:2 NKJV

O f all the discoveries I made in my pursuit of significance and purpose, the battlefront of the mind was the most eye-opening and enlightening. God used the truths revealed in this chapter to radically change my life and how I viewed the world forever. It was in the thought life where I experienced the greatest freedom. By God's gracious gift of His Son Jesus, my mind was honed into a weapon for His Kingdom.

God wants us to take charge of our thought life. God wants us to use our minds for His kingdom. He wants us to develop mental strength and a rock-solid character that reflects the change He made in us. Ultimately, He wants us to reflect His Son. Therefore, the battlefront of the mind is our primary fight as Lionheart Warriors. Our mission starts there. This battlefront will be a central to the fight. With the understanding that part of the enemy is inside of us, we will have good days and bad. There will be days where the fighting seems weak and other days where it seems fierce.

In the heart of our being, the flesh wars against the Spirit. Our fleshly mind wants to play tricks on us. Fear, doubt, insecurity, anxiety, temptations, all these attacks will come. They will come from within. Since they come from within, they will seem natural, as if they belong. The spiritual attacks will come as what seems like a friendly voice of reason. They will offer counsel and a weird sort of comfort. The flesh will use our imaginations to spiral our thoughts into a much deeper darkness. A snowball effect can take place in us and before we realize it, our emotions are triggered and off we go into a compounding spiral.

"Casting down imaginations, and every high thing that exalteth itself against the knowledge of God, and bringing into captivity every thought to the obedience of Christ"–2 Corinthians 10:5 KJV

We, as Lionheart Warriors, have a mandate to fight. We have a standing order to take the fight to the enemy and bring them into subjugation to Christ. These "imaginations" are not to roam freely in our heads. They are not to be given quarter and refuge. These thoughts are to be captured, exposed and brought into submission.

When left unchecked and unengaged, these thoughts and arguments against God's kingdom will pose the biggest risk to the Lionheart Warrior. They will fester. They will gain strength and a foothold in our minds. In this battlefront, the enemy is so close to the gates that we cannot afford to let the negative thoughts go free from confrontation. In life, all our actions and activities start in our minds. If the enemy can slow us down, set us off course or prevent us from living out God's call, they will be successful.

Looking back on our life prior to redemption, it is vital to understand and appreciate the role our minds played when we were enemies of God. It's easy to forget how our thoughts and emotions functioned to keep us locked at war with Him. In losing sight of that truth, we can be trapped and deceived in our new redeemed state while fighting God's battles going forward. The problem is we do not fully shake off the influence of our fallen self this side of eternity. The "old" man with all its hang ups and agendas, is still with us. It is there in the wings ready to pounce and send us headlong into our old ways. Its sole purpose is to thwart the advance of the Lionheart Warrior in the pursuit of victory.

"That he would grant you according to the riches of His Glory, to be strengthened with might through his Spirit in the inner man, that Christ may dwell in your hearts through faith; that you being rooted and grounded in love, may be able to comprehend with all the saints what is the width and length and depth and height— to know the love of Christ which passes knowledge; that you may be filled with all the fullness of God." –Ephesians 3:16-19 NKJV

Here, Paul shares how based in the love of Christ, we have access to God's power and influence through the deposit of Christ in our hearts. He says that He dwells there. So, we have two influences warring inside us for control. The "old" man and the spirit of Christ. It is only through faith that we are able to access God's provision. We must trustingly believe He is there and that He loves us. It is only by this faith we can begin to comprehend the love He has for us and in His love, there is unlimited power. The Faith component is a must-have, otherwise, we are only being influenced by the "old" man and its agenda.

"For God hath not given us the spirit of fear; but of power, and of love, and of a sound mind."
2 Timothy 1:7 KJV

This Spirit is brought into the fight by faith. Faith is a decision of the mind. We must make a conscious decision to believe this fact in order to access it. We cannot be double minded in our approach. We cannot be on the fence. We must go all in with this belief and in doing that, we are given His power. This is our fight in this battlefront, the fight for faith.

The "old" man will sow seeds of doubt. It will put forth questions of logic. At times, it will question the Lionheart Warrior's sanity with internal questions such as: "Are you being delusional?" "Isn't it all just make believe?" "Aren't you just doing this to make yourself feel better?" "Don't you feel childish and immature?"

We have to remember the "old" man is kindred to the Devil and in league with the other enemies. All the enemy works together on this. The "old" nature is a partner and cohort in rebellion, it is a liar aligned to the father of lies. The "old" man cannot be trusted. It knows its fate. Only at physical death will the carnal man be no more. So, our conflict with it continues until then. The flesh remains at war with the Spirit and we must rely on the Spirit over the flesh. This conscious reliance is the first battlefront of our involvement and it resides in the mind—our thoughts, desires and intentions are the battleground.

"Guard your Heart above all else, for it determines the course of your life." -Proverbs 4:23 NKJV

The heart is the seat of who we are and our motivations. All we do and desire starts at this point and flows out from there. The mind is central command for our personal fight campaign. If we cannot get the enemy out of our headquarters, how are we to ever take the fight to them in our other areas? Action must be taken. Steps must be made to combat these fleshly attacks. We must use the tools and training Almighty God has given us. All this by and through His Spirit and the instructions of His Word. We must ensure this mental battlefront is won and continues to be won day in and day out.

God has provided not only His Spirit, but the necessary instructions on how to move forward in securing personal victory. He has provided a full proof system for fortifying, pushing back and launching our own attacks on the enemy. All these instructions have been laid out and compiled in His war manual, the *Holy Bible*. We do not have to be discouraged or afraid when the attacks come, for He has given us all the necessary instructions.

"Be anxious for nothing, but in everything, by prayer and supplication, with thanksgiving, let your requests be made known to God; and the peace of God which surpasses

all understanding, will Guard your hearts and minds through Christ Jesus." -Philippians 4:7 NKJV

We are to guard our hearts and minds. This verse lays it out rather plainly. God says He is the one who does it. He offers us an exchange. He offers to step in and secure the victory in our place. He offers the way to thwart the enemy's attack in our mind. Surrender is the way to victory.

We are to give it to Him. We are to go to Him in prayer with thanksgiving. We are to be thankful for the opportunity to have Him intervene in our troubles. We are to appreciate His role in our fight. In exchange for us giving these issues over, He gives us His supernatural peace. We surrender our anxiety, fears, concerns and He gives us His peace. A peace that does not make earthly sense. A supernatural sense of peace that "guards our hearts and minds through Christ." Powerful!

The more we realize the nature of the war we are locked into, the less we will be caught off guard by these attacks. In the Basic Training section of this book, we learned that the armor of God needs to be used in all areas, especially the battlefront of the mind.

> *The flesh knows if it can get us to see the fight from its perspective, we will get discouraged and potentially give up.*

The enemy likes to attack us in very personal ways to our life and to our past. The flesh likes to sow seeds of doubt and confusion in our beliefs, our sense of self and in our intentions. It will assault our motivations and how we measure up as Lionheart Warriors. It will even try and question how well we are performing for the Kingdom of God.

When the enemy attempts to infiltrate our mind with seeds of doubt, it is hoping to stifle our progress. When attacking our performance, it is hoping to give us pause, slow us down and eventually quit. The flesh knows if it can get us to see the fight from its perspective, we will get discouraged and potentially give up. That is even more true when we experience failure. If the flesh can get us to focus on our defeats and setbacks, we may just fatigue of the fight. We may just slow down or take a break from the action, thus killing our momentum. God's armor is perfect in these spots.

"And let us not grow weary while doing good, for in due season we shall reap if we do not lose heart."
Galatians 6:9 NKJV

This is where God's helmet of salvation comes in. It is labeled "salvation" because salvation is ultimate victory. Ultimate victory is ultimate confidence. Salvation is the winner's circle after the race. Salvation is triumph and this triumph has been secured. Being hard pressed to convince a person they are a loser, the enemy will fail if said person already knows they have the victory. It would be foolish to even try. The winner's confidence is solid and belief in our outcome is unshakable. We were there. The experience was had. We were there when the game was won, so trying to suggest we lost is beyond ridiculous. Our victory is secured. We have already won the war through Christ. There is no arguing it. It's a done deal. The enemy will then be forced to switch tactics going forward. It will need to change its focus for future attacks.

Having failed to challenge our results, our flesh may try and attack our actual efforts in the war. It may feel inclined to point out our flaws and our inability to fight effectively. It may suggest we are the weakest link in God's army and that we do not belong. The enemy may try and suggest we are not worthy and that we really just drag our side down. It may try and convince us we are the least of all God's warriors. It is here, the breastplate of righteousness comes into play.

Our status in the history of this war is secured. Our identity, how we are viewed and how we will be viewed is firmly established in heaven. We have been declared righteous. We have been declared top performer. We have been declared and understood to be the best and most effective because we are in Christ. He is all those things and those things have been supernaturally applied to us. His righteousness is ours. His right standing is ours. His grace applies this truth. It's done, over and settled.

> *"But now the righteousness of God apart from the law is revealed, being witnessed by the Law and the Prophets, even the righteousness of God, through faith in Jesus Christ, to all and on all who believe. For there is no difference;"*
> *Romans 3:21-22 NKJV*

Every piece of armor is covered and reinforced by faith. To apply the breastplate in the battlefront of our mind, we must enact it by faith. God's grace enables it. The other pieces of His armor are used in much the same way. All is accomplished through relying on God's ways and provision and not on our own. This is how ground will be won in this war.

The Lionheart Warrior does not fight using the faulty power of the flesh, but that of the Spirit. We do not look to our understanding of these things, but to the truths God has given us in His word. We do not take the fight to the enemy in a fleshly way, but God's way. It is through releasing God's finished works in faith-filled prayer, we dominate the the battlefront of the mind. In doing all this, we receive the benefits Almighty God provides ahead of time. The battle of our mind is central to all other areas the Lionheart Warrior will face. Mindset and Belief are where it all begins. If this is area is not secured, the other areas will ultimately fall. The effects of this fall will be felt from our jobs, to our friendships, to our family, to our marriages and even to our own bodies. Since the mind is the launching point for all or actions, we must train it to the fullest.

Let us therefore renew our minds.

Chapter 12
The Forged Body

There was a season in my life where my insecurities and fears manifested as worry and concern over my physical health. Oddly enough, it first came over me while attending classes to become an EMT for the local fire department. The more I learned about all the conditions and situations that could kill someone, the more thoughts of death and doom that came over me. I became obsessed with all the potential diseases and conditions I could secretly die from. In that torturous season of my life, my mind played horrible tricks on me with worries of death and despair. This health obsession lasted for a season. By God's grace, my insecurities finally shifted back to their old home of insignificance and purposelessness once again.

It is important to understand the role the body plays in the fight for God's glory here on earth. Physical death and decay are an inescapable reality. We are going to get older. We are going to get weaker. We are going to get sick and we are going to eventually die. That is just the way it is. This reality is hard to swallow. The enemy can use this fact to really put a real black cloud on our successes and accomplishments in our minds. It can cause our efforts in things deemed important or vital to be questioned. This attitude can almost get to the point of being, "What's the point?" "Why even bother?" In reality, the truth of the matter is, those questions are not exactly wrong.

Follow me for a minute.

If the whole point of this life is for our own glory, then those questions make perfect sense. If it's all about our time here and our own appeasement, then the question of what does it matter and what is the point is valid. It will all be lost anyway, right? If there is no consciousness past the grave, then the moment we take our last breath, any memory of it vanishes as well. To us, it will be like nothing ever really happened. That last breath comes to us all, some years from now, others sooner. The end is absolute for all.

> *"Therefore, whether you eat or drink or whatever you do, do all to the glory of God." -1 Corinthians 10:31 NKJV*

> *I beseech you therefore, brethren, by the mercies of God, that you present your bodies as a living sacrifice, holy, acceptable to God, which is your reasonable service." -Romans 12:1 NKJV*

As these two verses make very clear, the point is God's glory. Struggling to honor Him with our bodies and making all our efforts be for His kingdom is the ultimate point. Whether we can do it for a minute, a day or six decades, it all needs to be about Him. Looking back at our original questions of the purposefulness, the answer is quite resounding, His glory. This is the reason we are to "bother" in all of it. He wants it, He demands it and He deserves it.

Lionheart Warriors must look at all areas of our lives as tools and areas of striving forth for God's glory. It must be our singular focus. It must be our overall mission statement. Using what God has given us to extract the most glory for Him is what truly motivates the Lionheart Warrior. It is the idea of pushing oneself in this physical reality in such a way that we must rely on God's supernatural provision to be successful. When we slip up, we must come to His throne of grace, gather His strength and get back after it. Knowing deep down that it is not us doing it, but Him doing it through us.

We are to be stewards of our bodies. We have been given an amazing vessel to accomplish things. We have been entrusted with a complex machine to do the bidding of our minds and wills.

Jesus tells a story of a landowner who loans out differing amounts of money to three different men, each with the understanding that they are to multiply the investment before the owner returns from a long trip.

Upon the owner's return, he calls these three men before him to give account of their efforts. Two of the men doubled the initial investment, while the third man buried his investment for safe keeping. Rewards were given to the first two diligent workers and punishment to the third who buried the investment. Like all of Jesus' parables, they speak to a higher moral and spiritual truth. The workers were to be responsible and diligent with the owner's money entrusted to them. They were going to be held accountable. There was going to be a moment where their efforts, or lack of effort, would be evaluated and measured.

Just as with the servants in Jesus' parable, we have been given talents from Him. We have been given areas of operation in this life, areas of responsibility. Just like the servants in the story, we are accountable to God for how these talents are invested. We are not to bury them or, worse yet, destroy them. We are to double their value. We are to get as much gain from the Lord's investment as possible. We are not meant to ride it out selfishly, but multiply it, and then we can give it back as an offering of worship and homage to the Source of our being, very similar to the parable.

One of these investments is our physical body. Unfortunately, most people do not view their body in this light. By default, we are slothful and lazy. We are selfish and only interested in pursuing our own selfish pleasure. This attitude is from the "old" nature, the flesh. It is an inherent part of our former rebellious selves.

In our natural selfishness, God's glory becomes unrecognizable by us. We only see how discipline and hardship affects us negatively. We only see difficulty and uncomfortableness as taking away from our time and perceived sense of happiness. In that selfish state, we do not really understand that discipline is the manifestation of a living sacrifice life-style. In this lifestyle, we receive true joy and true pleasure from the Lord. The slothful lazy side of us has an opposite side that is equally offensive if not more so—body obsession.

Body obsession is an infatuation with one's health or body shape. It is a false idol and a form of self-worship. We strive to obtain a perfect body and or reach perfect health. This self-absorption can easily be passed off as admirable and lofty by outside observers, however, it is nothing more than arrogant self-glorification. We grind it out in training just "taking care of our bodies," but really we are doing it for our self image. We obsess with being fit, attractive and physically powerful, and all that for no other reason than self-aggrandizement. It becomes an addiction. Vanity. Idolatry. We get wrapped up using "healthy living" as a way to sacrifice ourselves on the altar of the god, self. We obsess about our looks, feelings, image and status to the point that we are trying to earn eternal life (longer life in our body) through, diet, lifestyle, meditation, sport, etc. It is self-worship, plain and simple. Foolishness. Despite our best efforts and strategies, our vessel will fatigue, falter and fade with nothing to show for it, but a life sacrificed on our very own altar.

The Lionheart Warrior must not fall into either of those two extremes. We know that in taking care of our body, it weaponizes us to fight longer, smarter and easier. When we avoid sickness, we avoid all the hang ups that come with sickness. We know that when we are in any kind of real pain or discomfort, it is hard to focus on anything else. We tend to struggle to think about anything else, besides our discomfort. That can pose a grave concern if we need to be about our King's business.

When we are in terrible physical shape, it can seriously hinder our ability to take advantage of service opportunities. Opportunities to serve other people come in all forms, some of which may require a fit and healthy body. Those type of service opportunities can require strenuous activity such as yard work or other types of physical labor. Having poor physical fitness hampers those efforts. Perhaps it leads to us passing up on good opportunities all together.

Obviously, this concept excludes those warriors who live with certain sicknesses and physical handicaps outside their control. We all know whether we truly fall into this category or not. A person who is unable to do things based on certain limitations is not required to steward them. God's Kingdom is not limited by our abilities. Each warrior will be accessed based on the "talents" God has given them. Jesus taught us when much is given to us, much is required from us. We are responsible for stewarding what the King gives us. We are not responsible for what was given to another. Similar to the parable, each warrior will answer for how their particular talents were used in the King's service.

We are responsible for stewarding what the King gives us.

It is equally important to understand the weaknesses of our bodies. Besides slowly wearing out and weakening, we must understand that our natural desires can be used against us. Our desire for food, clothing and drink can be used to motivate us in directions contrary to the mission of the King.

Our desires for shelter, sex and excitement can cause us to consider things that are in opposition to the glory of God. The enemy thrives on using our natural desires against us. The Devil, the world system and the fleshly self, all love to twist and misdirect our natural desires.

One of our greatest pitfalls and traps is our unchecked sexual desire. Struggles in the areas of lust and pornography plague humanity. The enemy has this area of temptation down to a science. The world system feeds it in modern entertainment and lifestyle. With the advent of the internet and smart phones, we have access to these temptations 24 hours a day, 7 days a week and 12 months out of the year.

The desire of the flesh is all-consuming. We are to be careful not to take it lightly or minimize those desires as unavoidable sin. Unchecked sexual expression is contrary to the King's orders and plans for His Kingdom, and will create havoc in the warrior's areas of operation. Learning how to keep in check the desires of the flesh is a useful

Kingdom discipline. The Lord has built into us essential tools to combat the desires of the flesh.

Fasting is a powerful tool for the Warrior in his training and fighting. In fasting, the warrior voluntarily denies gratification to certain natural desires of the body in order to bring all into submission to the King. Through prayer and fasting, the Lionheart Warrior brings those natural desires under control by leaning on the Spirit and not their flesh for strength. This is a spiritual discipline that requires constant reliance on the power of the Holy Spirit in order to be successful. Once cleared by a medical professional, the warrior can embark on various stints of prayer and fasting to discipline and bring the body into submission to the will.

As we can see, the battlefront of our body is vital to our cause. Understanding how the enemy attacks and the proper application of God's provisions are essential. By the grace of God through the power of prayer, fasting and by putting on His armor, the warrior will prevail. The body obeys the mind. The mind must be made to obey the Spirit. If there is a disconnect in any of these areas, it will be felt in our battlefront and the other AOs will be put in serious jeopardy.

The Lionheart Warrior must be disciplined and rely on the King. It is through God's process that progress will be made. Having secured the inner ring, we have a foundation to push into the middle ring of our AO. We must examine how our personhood connects and interacts with others. By looking at our relationships, we will gain insight into our deeper purpose, strengths and vulnerabilities in the fight for God's glory.

Let us push on to victory.

SECTION IV
MIDDLE RING

CHAPTER 13
SECURING THE CASTLE

There is no way to avoid it; no man is an island. No man can walk this earth alone. We were designed to live in a community and to interact with one another as a group. Within our soul, we need close connections with other people. We need those bonds to feel complete, balanced and have purpose. We have major influence on those we surround ourselves with and they have influence on us. It is here where the battles will be made. This is the relational battlefront.

In this ongoing war for God's glory, His design for community is under constant attack from the enemy. The enemy knows relationships and personal connections are important and it will take every opportunity to maximize the damage relational conflict can create. It is our role as Lionheart Warriors to glorify God by protecting, securing and strengthening the bonds between us. In doing so, we take the fight to the enemy.

The dark forces know they do not have to attack the Lionheart Warrior directly, but can attack through those relationships that are in close proximity. They know we have strong emotional attachments and will get bogged down and focused on those closet to us. Through these strong emotional connections, we are heavily swayed good or bad.

As part of their overall strategy, the enemy counts on the fact that we take attacks to our loved ones very personally. They know it provides a conduit to our mind. They know despite our strongest resistances, family and friends provide easy access into our inner ring. Especially so with those strong and hardened warriors who have their Personal Area of Operation locked down and secure, the enemy must use alternate means to wreak havoc.

Our middle ring or, relational area of operation, consists of three battlefronts: marriage, children and social circles. These battlefronts make up our primary relationships in life. They are the personal AOs linked to the world.

Two of the three components of our relational AO are easily definable by God's Word. Despite the influence by the world system in its assault on Truth, marriage is defined as consisting between one man and one woman. In the chapter that follows on marriage, we will discuss how children play into our AOs and see the different forms they can take.

As for social circles, that will take a bit more clarifying. When it comes to social circles, it can include a friend, an acquaintance, an associate or affiliate. These are the people who have influence over the warrior, but are not immediate family. Extended family can definitely fit into the category of social circle.

In the age of social media, social circles have become even more complicated. Those individuals who would have had zero influence on us 20 years ago, now have substantial impact through interactions, good and bad, over social media. In modern times, our "neighborhoods" have radically changed. They now include individuals we only interact with over a digital device through short written communiques.

For warriors who are not married or do not have children, those two areas are vacant in the relational AO. The social circle incorporates those relationships that are not quite marriage, but carry a heavy influence on the warrior. As we study the marriage front, we will examine the spiritual aspect of what happens when a fiancé becomes a wife or husband and why those who exist outside that bond are not interchangeable. God's directions on the matter are very specific and we will examine the spiritual importance of the marriage designation.

The relational AO is the second layer to the Lionheart Warrior's domain. These are the first stages that exist outside our personal AO, and therefore carry the most potential for creating honor or dishonor.

They are the first line of influence we have and will be the most challenging in this conflict. They provide us with a great litmus test for our efforts and how well we are following the path God has laid before us.

As Lionheart Warriors, we must have our personal AO secure and in order because any problems we have will spill over into our other areas. Our ability to tend and secure within our relationships is paramount to success and will have a direct impact on the war. Due to the link between our personal and our territorial areas, the relational provides opportunity for both good and the bad to occur in our lives. The enemy knows all too well the residual influence each AO holds and plans to exploit it however they can. No area is isolated unto itself. Given long enough, the areas of our life are all connected and if one falls, the rest are susceptible. We must remain in a constant state of vigilance. We must be accessing all the fronts for vulnerability. Our enemy is determined and crafty in its approach. At first chance, it will use our spiritual pride and complacency to infiltrate our areas.

It is only through humble reliance on God's grace and provision we will be able to see success and avoid failure. We have been built for relationships and in them, we bring the most glory to God and push His Kingdom agenda. It starts with those closet and most precious to us. Let us take the fight to the enemy, putting them on their heels, so that they do not get the slightest foothold.

Be on guard, for the enemy is at the gates!

CHAPTER 14
THE IRON BOND

"And for this reason a man shall leave his father and mother and be joined to his wife, and the two shall become one flesh." -Matthew 19:5 NKJV

This is probably the hardest chapter to write about as a husband. One cannot help but feel like a hypocrite when trying to share the "shoulds" and "should nots" of marriage. Marriage is probably the number one area a Lionheart Warrior will be the most vulnerable outside their personal AO. One only has to live in this world a short while to realize that marriage is a favorite target of the enemy. The marriage relationship is surrounded and saturated by emotion. It is an area where the enemy can create the most turmoil and hardship in our lives. This area produces the most heartache and strife in the life of the warrior. One of the quickest ways to send the warrior off mission is to cause trouble between the Lionheart Warrior and their spouse.

In conventional warfare, it is a very effective strategy to attack the home front of the army you are at war with. If you can get their soldiers to worry about the safety of their wives and children, you can divide their minds on the battlefield and make them worry about home. If a soldier's mind is constantly set back to the rear with his family and not on the mission, he can not only put himself in danger, but his entire unit. Our enemy uses the same basic strategy in this war. Unlike in conventional war, our enemy understands the supernatural bond that exists between husband and wife. It understands marriage goes well beyond just two people in a committed relationship.

The supernatural mystery of husbands and wives being one flesh is at the heart of understanding this battlefront. The marriage relationship is unique in all of God's creation. It has greater significance than two people being shacked up or under some sort of romantic commitment. There is a bond ordained by God and transcends human understanding.

You see, the enemy knows it cannot ultimately influence us directly in our inner being once we have been sealed by the Spirit of God. It must attack from the outside in. Upon redemption, the Devil and his angels lost power over us. They cannot control us directly anymore. If the enemy cannot attack us directly, it will use elements and situations from the outside to get the job done. Marriage relations offer the enemy the most bang for the buck. This approach works for the enemy because of the unique connection between a husband and wife. Causing turmoil in that spiritual relationship can produce major results. This turmoil, no matter how slight, can stifle the efforts and motivation of the warrior. The enemy's mission is simply to make a warrior's marriage a liability instead of an asset in the fight for God's glory.

Have you ever wondered why marriage is such an important target of the enemy? Think about all the failed marriages that exist in our society. Think about the devastation that is left in their wake. There is a ripple effect felt for generations. It can destroy whole cultures. Think about the years of pain and anguish felt by children of broken marriages. It's an epidemic. The devastation doesn't stop at the natural, it goes deep into to the spiritual as well.

According to God's word, the covenant marriage is a physical, tangible manifestation of God's relationship with His people. It is to be the earthly model of God's connection with us. It a representation of the bond between Christ and His bride, the Church. These spiritual bonds cannot be witnessed with our natural eyes, so Almighty God has chosen to have marriage reflect these truths to the world. Marriage is to be the point of reference to understand the relationship between God and mankind. It points out the duties and responsibilities each side has in covenant relationship—how to love, protect, provide, be in fellowship and show honor to each other. It is designed to reflect the living testimony of those truths.

> *Marriage is to be the point of reference to understand the relationship between God and mankind.*

As humans, we are always looking for ways to improve our marriages. We are looking for ways to strengthen the bond between us. The Lionheart Warrior only needs to look to the standard of God in His person. His role as husband to His people provides us with all the answers to what an effective marriage looks like.

At this point, it becomes glaringly obvious why the enemy wants to destroy this spiritual symbol. If the enemy can wreak havoc and tarnish marriage, it will send the message that God's "symbol" is a reflection of the disorder and chaos between God and man. The representation is a complete failure. Now making any reference to God as "husband" is an insult and corrupted. Any reference to our bond with Him as "marriage" is tainted, never to be trusted or received with any sincerity. Any mention of the marriage relationship being holy or sacred falls on deaf ears. As if that is not bad enough, the enemy takes things one step farther.

The enemy knows it can be more effective in undermining God's glory by making the man's side in the relationship be the chief reason for the downfall of marriage. It wants the man's side of the relationship to be the one ultimately at fault. It wants the masculine male side to be the destroyer of this spiritual relationship. In this way, the enemy gets to kill two birds with one stone. It gets to go after the God side of the relationship, because the man represents God in this symbol. The husband is the manifestation of God's duties and responsibilities in the covenant relationship. If you can have men be the primary reason for the downfall of marriage, well you get extra points in your attempts to tarnish God's glorious image.

If the husband is the example of God and Christ's side of the relationship, then you have a conscious and subconscious way of undermining thoughts of God in people's minds. They now have a tainted point of reference for God. You can undercut the idea of Him as a husband. You can hamper any mental connection the people have to a loving, sacrificing, providing, protecting God. Talk about psychological warfare on a whole nother level.

The world system has joined in and launched a full-on assault against the idea of men, manhood and what it means to be in a covenant marriage. If you stop to consider, it makes perfect sense and is consistent with the enemy's overall goals. Conducting these operations accomplishes so much more toward the primary goal of dismantling God's glory. Every failed marriage, broken man and broken woman becomes just one more example of the failure of doing things God's way. It is a direct reflection on God and His nature. Given the gravity of a failed marriage, it makes sense when God says in His word that He hates divorce.

Knowing how high the stakes are in this area of the war, it is imperative the Lionheart Warrior be vigilant. We must be methodical in our approach to marriage. We must be systematic in our understanding of the roles in the relationship. We must be intentional in our plans, words and deeds with our spouse. Marriage is a representation and a direct form of worship toward God.

This responsibility is of utmost importance. There is no other way around it. We as Lionheart Warriors must step up to the challenge. We must answer the call to take back our marriages and make right the wrongs of the past. We must push the enemy from the gates. It is vital that we understand our roles and the orders the King has given in these particular areas. The Apostle Paul provides plenty of insight into the roles going forward.

"Husbands, love your wives, even as Christ also loved the church, and gave himself for it;" Ephesians 5:25 KJV

If you give this command from scripture any real thought, you will realize just how difficult it is as a standard. Husbands are to view their wives as Christ viewed His church. She is the object of His affection and His redeeming mission. The same attitude of redemptive sacrifice Jesus had for His people, Lionheart Warriors are to have for their wives. Is there a higher level of selfless love? Is there any role more difficult? Can this even be pulled off?

If you know anything about Jesus at all, you understand the gravity of His love for His people. You see the vastness of the lengths to which He would go to save and restore them. There have been tens of thousands of books written on the subject. There have been millions of sermons preached on this concept alone.

The orders laid down for husbands is not a cutesy little sticker for one's car. It's not a quippy sound bite or quote for a t-shirt. This mandate is scary. Think about this. What if all your arguments and disagreements must be filtered through this mandate from God? What if husbands have no grounds to argue their side of any discussion, no matter the offense or gravity unless they are meeting this most basic requirement.

Love your wife just like Jesus loved the Church.

If you are anything like me, you want to yell out, "So unfair...Who can win?"

I am not sure exactly, but that may be the larger point. It's a suicide mission of pure self-sacrifice on the husband's part.

I can just hear the discussion now:

"So you want to get married huh?"

"Let me tell you a little-known requirement of God's having to do with being a husband."

Ouch!

> *"Wives, submit yourselves unto your own husbands, as*
> *unto the Lord."*
> *Ephesians 5:22 KJV*

The husband is the divinely designated leader of the marriage. He is given authority to lead and cover his bride. It is rather difficult to lead one who is not willing to follow. God lays out in this verse the duty of the wife in the marriage. As a Lionheart Warrior, we are to work as unto the Lord. We are to obey as unto the Lord. It goes without saying, this is not a license for allowing of abuse and oppression. God sets this standard in place with the understanding there are chains of authority in all organizations and they must be followed or chaos will ensue.

We can see how this standard for wives has been abused by a fallen world. That is a testament to the deception of the enemy. So much so, that even quoting this truth from God can illicit cringes from some hearers. The enemy has really done a work in our world where we feel we must take the time to justify His will and commands in order for them be received with joy.

In the end of the day, God knows men are not Jesus and are in need of His grace. He knows they are not capable in their own power to operate like Him. He knows they will fail miserably. He knows and He cares deeply. He knows none of this makes any sense from a worldly perspective and is actually counter intuitive. He knows the idea of it all looks too far-fetched to even attempt apart from Him. He knows all of that and yet He smiles. He smiles, because He knows we will have to rely on Him. Husbands and wives alike. He knows we will have to seek His patience and wisdom. He knows we will have to trust Him. He knows we will have to have faith, not in our ability to be like Christ, but in His ability to make our mistakes right; His power to take our faults and turn them right so that at the end of the day, He is glorified. Glorified not in our ability to check that box, but glorified in being worked out through us.

Men need to examine what it means to love their wives like Christ, and women need to examine what it means to hold their husbands in reverence—what it means to choose love beyond emotion, beyond beauty, beyond pleasure and beyond pride. The Lionheart Warrior must see the heart of his master to get an idea of the lengths and depths love goes. We must learn from the Master, if we are to have any hope in this war. We must study Him. We must see how He loves. We must see how He handles all the different types of people He came into contact with, how He handled all the different personalities, problems and variables. We must see how He spoke and the words He used. We must see the spirit of His responses. We are to always study His example. Our understanding of His training doesn't stop this side of eternity.

We are to take our understanding into the areas of our lives and attempt to apply the lessons. We make corrections and move forward all the while understanding His grace fuels and moves us. It is through our obedience that His grace is released to us. We act on what we learn from Him and His power is available. It was already there. We simply had to take hold of it through faith, knowing that we are doing His work in our marriage.

This war requires constant fellowship with Him. It requires death to self, daily. It requires constant intercession on behalf of our spouses and to request strength and insight in how to proceed on our respective paths. The enemy will tempt us to give up. The enemy will tempt us to become frustrated and bitter. The enemy will tempt us to think there is another way. It has been doing that from the very beginning. Just like with Adam in the garden, the enemy will try and convince us it's everyone's fault but our own. He will have husbands blame their wives and wives blame their husbands. He will even try and convince us that God is ultimately at fault.

In the end, we have to humble ourselves, seek God and love our wives and revere our husbands. This is a lifelong pursuit not to be taken lightly. The stakes are high, not only in the supernatural, but also in the material around us. Conflict is a constant reality. The fight will be brutal at times. The objectives will seem impossible. No matter how bad it gets, know that God has grace available. He honors this campaign. He designed this campaign and He has the answer to its victory. Trust Him and stand firm.

Love leads the way!

CHAPTER 15
BUILDING THE LEGACY

"As a father shows compassion to his children, so the Lord shows compassion to those who fear him."
Psalms 103:13 ESV

There is an all-out assault on the concept of fatherhood. The world has relegated the role of a father to a wage earner and sperm donor. He has been shoved aside and marginalized leaving obvious devastation in the wake. The concept of father has become the punchline in jokes. Fatherhood has been rallied against at protests. Social media and television consistently portray men not only in an unfavorable light, but as bumbling idiots or clueless morons who must be sidestepped and outright manipulated by everyone in the family. The father is seen as a necessary evil by modern society and we are seeing the damaging effects this paradigm is having.

These concepts are foreign to the biblical understanding of the father. The Lionheart Warrior loathes these images of the sex crazed, mentally numb, clueless man-child the world portrays as a father. The Lionheart Warrior knows the enemy is in full assault mode on the family unit. We understand the deeper spiritual war going on and the enemy's ultimate goal to portray Almighty God as incompetent.

Throughout the *Bible*, the Lord describes Himself has a father. He does this not so that mankind can have a model to understand Him, but so we have a model to understand ourselves. He is the standard, not the other way around. He invented our roles and duties, not us. Simply, Lionheart Warrior men are to be father models in His likeness. He was a father long before man was. The true concept of fatherhood was fashioned after His role, His duties and His attributes. He is the archetype. He is the standard for all that a true and authentic father should be.

The enemy knows God is Father. It is intimately familiar with His self-designation and design. It knows the Lord made men to be image bearers of that fact. Earthly fathers were designed to be a physical, tangible manifestation of the fatherhood of God. He was designed after God Himself. As an object lesson to better understand God as Father, man was created. Basically, men are finite, inferior signs pointing to the ultimate Father in heaven. Tarnish the example and you can distort understanding of the genuine article.

The undermining of the family, and in particular the role of father, is near and dear to the battle plan of the enemy. It knows that if it can destroy the idea of fatherhood, it can steal truth and glory from God. If it can make fathers look ridiculous, it can mar the conceptual image of the Father in people's minds. If it can make fathers out to be powerless clowns only serving a support function in the family unit, it can make understanding truth next to impossible. With the concept of father destroyed, the enemy can cause a rift between the minds of men and the Lord. All masculine problems in society are a direct result of the fall, and testify to the spiritual war being waged all around us.

The Lionheart Warrior's role is to not only represent God the Father tangibly in our own relationships, but also to push back against this satanic trend of the world system attempting to redefine fatherhood. By representing fatherhood as God designed it, the Lionheart Warrior fulfills God's intentions, while simultaneously undermining the agenda of the enemy. The warrior's fatherhood mandate is to restore the role and right understanding of man's position in the family unit. They are tasked daily to combat the messages and effects of the world. We are to be the righteous alternative to the false narrative being sold by the enemy in society.

By operating in accordance with God's design, those individuals outside the family unit become enlightened and inspired to do the same.

A Lionheart Warrior living up to their role as father will have a major impact outside the scope of his own family, but will also inspire other men to seek out God's truth of fatherhood. By following this mandate, a residual effect is created which by God's grace turns back the tide initiated by the enemy. In so doing, more and more men will lead their families for the Kingdom.

> *A Lionheart Warrior living up to their role as father will have a major impact outside the scope of his own family, but will also inspire other men to seek out God's truth of fatherhood.*

When a man starts to fulfill his role and position as father, he will see fruit produced in the relational area of operation. This new path will impact the warrior's children for generations to come. It will have a compounding effect in more ways than can be understood by finite limited minds. The power of the Spirit will intervene to reinforce, support and encourage this true concept of fatherhood in their families' minds. They will have a rock-solid example before them pointing to that higher entity. As the children's concept of father changes for the better, their minds are ripe for direct understanding of their heavenly Father.

It is important to remember attacks are sure to come. As the enemy perceives ground lost in this area, it will attempt to gain something back. We are to expect an increase in attacks and resistance to this operation. Relying on the Lord through faith, obedience and prayer will keep the warrior on the proper path. God always provides provision for the tasks assigned.

The heavenly Father longs for warriors to reflect His glory in fatherhood. Wisdom to pursue these objectives are readily available upon request. As with any mission and fight, we will make mistakes and fail to stand firm in the role in which we are placed. The warrior must acknowledge his shortcomings and go before the King for renewal and fresh provision once again to get back in the fight. It is through that daily prayer and in-depth study of the attributes of God as Father the warrior will see the mistakes made and the corrections to be made.

> *"Train up a child in the way he should go: and when he is old, he will not depart from it."*
> *Proverbs 22:6 KJV*

Jesus demonstrated a special place in his heart for children while walking the earth. He understood how vulnerable and impressionable they were. Some of His most stark warnings revolved around the harm done to children. He spoke of a grim fate for those individuals who caused any harm to children. He went so far as to warn that leading them down a wrong path will result in dire eternal consequences. He warned His disciples over and over to think about the effects our actions had on children. Lionheart Warriors know the King's warnings apply to all children, especially those entrusted to us in our families.

> *"And you, fathers, do not provoke your children to wrath, but bring them up in the training and admonition of the Lord."*
> *Ephesians 6:4 NKJV*

The way a father raises his children will stay with them for a lifetime. It will impact how they go on to raise and influence their own children. Over the years, there are have been numerous studies and surveys done addressing the negative influence a toxic father has on children. Ask any man willing to share about his problems and issues and it is almost guaranteed to center around his relationship with his father. Prisons are full of broken men who either had no relationship or a horrible relationship with their father. It is a known fact that men who lead the most destructive, vile lives in our society overwhelmingly came from fatherless homes. The enemy is waging a very effective campaign against fatherhood. Since men are falling for it hook, line and sinker, women are having to burn the candle at both ends. They are having to stand in the gap and take up the slack left by the absence of real men.

In the battle for our children, women are having to take on dual roles to get the job done. They inherently know that their children need the influence of the father, so they either try to fulfill a role they were not designed for or they bring in a substitute.

The Lionheart Warrior understands the battle for the children is a complex front and cannot be addressed haphazardly. The stakes for failure and defeat are far too high. Motherhood in many cases has become a dual venture of both father and mother. Given that is the case, women are not able to reach their full potential as a mother. They are divided. Their energies are splintered and they become exhausted and frustrated, all this is then felt by the children. Being forced to take on double duty, the mother constantly feels overwhelmed and stretched to the point of breaking. Through God's grace, a mother who finds herself in a position without a father for her children will find the strength and power needed.

> *"A father of the fatherless, a defender of widows, Is God in His holy habitation."*
> *Psalms 68:5 NKJV*

This verse speaks to the heart of God in these situations. He becomes the father to the fatherless and the defender to the husbandless. Just like we saw in the previous chapter, God uses the roles of husband and father to point to Himself. He designed these positions to be a reflection on Him and His glory. He takes it very serious how those roles are portrayed and carried out.

The enemy knows God's heart and desire in this area and therefore makes every attempt to undermine it. The Lionheart Warrior must push the enemy from the gates. It is time that men of God wake up. It is time for fathers to stand up for their kids and mothers to unite with the fathers. It is time for us to become the Lionheart Warriors God designed us to be. This requires commitment. This requires conviction and discipline. This requires patience and wisdom. The enemy will send everything against us in this particular area. Expect resistance from every direction.

Do not be surprised if people who would normally be very supportive of biblical things come out against you. Do not be shocked if resistance comes from those most benefiting from a right role of fatherhood. Change is a tough pill to swallow and the world system has brain washed most people against these truths.

Through prayer and putting on God's armor daily, the battle will be won. God highly honors those looking to represent Him on this earth. God blesses those who strive to be what He designed them to be. God will always equip those warriors to stand up and charge forward in this fight for His Glory.

The time is now to take back the family.

CHAPTER 16
MAXIMIZING INFLUENCER

"A man who has friends must himself be friendly, But there is a friend who sticks closer than a brother."
Proverbs 18:24 NKJV

We are social creatures. We are built for relationships. We are always looking for ways to connect and influence others in this life. Some of life's most powerful influences are in our social circles. Even beyond childhood, social or peer pressure is still a powerful motivating force. We want people to enjoy our company. We want for people to hold us in high regard and respect us. Deep down, we all want to be connected to others in some way. God has quite a bit to say about the company we choose to keep.

According to God's word, picking the right social circle can mean the difference between prosperity and poverty. Associating with the right crowd can mean either a life of peace or one of constant conflict. The right group can mean an existence grounded in wisdom or an existence of walking after foolishness. An old saying goes something like this, "Show me your friends and I will show you your future."

"As iron sharpens iron, So a man sharpens the countenance of his friend."
Proverbs 27:17 NKJV

We are a product of our affiliations. We are the result of those individuals we allow to influence us. The concept is easy to understand, but sometimes very hard to implement in any practical way. Our friends and family have a strong power over us. We acquired them over many years and they represent many different experiences. Those influencers are sometimes as much a part of our lives as our closest family members. In some circumstances, these individuals can be our only real family and their influence is more than apparent in our lives.

The Lionheart Warrior understands the power of social relationships and how they affect our overall contentment in life. We understand these relationships are not meant to be taken lightly or flippantly. They affect our sense of wellbeing and cause issues well beyond the area they actually touch. Having a poor understanding of their power can be a liability in more ways than one.

The enemy knows all-too-well the power these relationships have over us. It knows the emotions attached to these connections and the weight they carry. It knows the gravity of their influence in the lives of the warrior, and the enemy will take intentional steps to exploit these strong influencers.

Since the beginning of time, the enemy has mastered the art of using our relationships to manipulate and meet the evil agenda. It will exploit whatever can be used to attack and sidetrack the mission. Despite best efforts, the Devil and his angels cannot attack the Lionheart Warrior directly due to the presence of the Holy Spirit in us. Direct internal attack is difficult, so the enemy will use our close social connections and relationships to get to us.

> "Ye are of God, little children, and have overcome them: because greater is he that is in you, than he that is in the world." 1 John 4:4 KJV"

Therefore, the Devil has to use those who do not have the Holy Spirit to influence us negatively. We are speaking about those social connections that are not in the Kingdom. To be clear, these individuals are still consciously or subconsciously fighting against our King. They are still linked directly to the enemy and still in line with its plans and mission. The longest war is still going on and these people have not been rescued yet. They are continuing the fight against God's Kingdom and most of that time without even realizing or acknowledging it.

The Lionheart Warrior must not be naive about these spiritual realities. We must understand the deep connection we have to these individuals and the potential dangers those connections pose. They can make our mission more difficult. Despite our desire to be in relationships with them, we must not lose focus of our true mission to glorify God and take the fight to the enemy. This is our chief end. As part of that end, we are on a constant lookout for opportunities to share the life-altering good news that led to our freedom—the saving news of Christ and His redeeming love. We can be the one to bring the greatest news to their lives—the message of their divine deliverance.

The influence we carry over our social relationships is far greater than the negative influence they may have over us, all due to the supernatural empowerment provided by the Holy Spirit. We are equipped by His Spirit to share the good news of the King's rescue and redemption. Despite the good news, this sharing can cause conflict inside the relationship.

As we start bringing our focus toward the King's call for our lives, these individuals may sense a slight change in our motives in the relationship. The enemy will increase resistance to our influence over them. It will be no surprise if the once-close affiliations start to distance themselves from the warrior. They will notice this new perspective from us and they will potentially avoid future interactions altogether.

It's important to note, this resistance and avoidance should not be because of an aggressive over-bearing onslaught on our friends. Rescue operations are to be done through love and grace, not through abrasive coercion. Those distancing themselves will do so from being spiritually uncomfortable, not socially uncomfortable. This will cause them to want to remove themselves from our spiritual influence or possibly even launch passive aggressive jabs and attacks on us. There becomes a crisis of conscience which can reveal their internal strife.

"The wicked flee when no one pursues, but the righteous are as bold as a lion." Proverbs 28:1 NKJV

The Lionheart Warrior must stay strong to convictions while exercising compassion toward these relationships who are lost and blind by their situation. The King has given us an example of compassion through His word in dealing with those still lost. He loves them dearly. His heart burns for them and, as Spirit-filled Lionheart Warriors, ours should as well. The flesh will try and use these conflicts to tempt the warrior into becoming self-righteous.

A word of caution, self-righteousness in us can lead to an inflated sense of ourselves. We can start acting as if we earned our new status and therefore can lord it over those still lost and blind. A spiritual arrogance happens to new warriors all the time and can even be a proof of false conversion. Be warned!

The Lionheart Warrior has an obligation to not only surround themselves with Kingdom brothers and sisters, but to influence all for the King.

The false warrior is rampant in our churches today. Self-righteousness is a cancer in churches and should be rallied against by all true followers. It is a deception by the enemy in order to undermine the cause of the Kingdom. Self-righteousness provides propaganda to the other side in the war and creates a counter argument to claims of conversion. The key thing to remember is our focus on the mission and the grace given by our King. This focus requires an intimate understanding of His plan and purposes; plans for fighting this war in our social relationships that can only be accomplished and sustained through prayer and study of His word.

The Lionheart Warrior has an obligation to not only surround themselves with Kingdom brothers and sisters, but to influence all for the King. By actively pursuing ways to share the good news in our social circles, we are on mission. We need a methodical approach in order to accomplish tasks associated with sharing the good news in all circumstances. Therefore, we must be intentional and our approach well thought out. We will need to pray and be prayed over continuously with utilization of God's armor. Knowing the enemy will be on the offensive at all times in this area, we must stay prepared and ready.

"Behold I send you out as sheep in the midst of wolves. Therefore be wise as serpents and as harmless as doves."
Matthew 10:16 NKJV

The territory is hostile. We are fighting a war where the enemy does not want to lose one more battle or soul to our side. Every soul freed from its bondage is another blow to that cosmic ego. The most harmless social setting can be a fierce spiritual battleground. Every word and deed shared has a vital spiritual component. We must not be naive about our role in these interactions. The warrior knows the littlest things have major influence on our relationships' personal conversion and nothing we say or do should be taken for granted. This fight is in the spiritual realm.

The Lionheart Warrior must remain in constant reliance on the Spirit in prayer. The battle we are engaged in is a spiritual one and at face value it may appear to be a battle we are personally losing. By the worldly material standards, something can be categorized as a win, but actually be a loss in the spiritual. For instance, a warrior could win an argument, but lose the one they are arguing with. We may be right in the truth we expressed, but in our style, push the person farther away. On the flip side, something can be a triumph spiritually but come at a personal loss. We could have made a positive dent spiritually, but have been personally ridiculed in the process. We must learn to see things from a truly different perspective.

We are always looking to plant seeds for God's Kingdom. We live a life of service to the King in all areas of our lives and pray the Holy Spirit reveals the truth to those within our social sphere. We actively engage in efforts to rescue our friends. We take every opportunity, no matter how small, to influence them for Christ. Winning them over does not consist of pointing out their flaws and lording over their failures, but the testifying to the power of the King in our lives. The Spirit guides and directs the warrior in this effort. We must rely on His strength and His promptings and not on our own.

At the end of the day, these relationships are finite. Like all other areas of our life, they are to be a catalyst for glorifying God on earth. We are to be pursuing His plans and purposes in all things. This pursuit includes bringing as many people over to His Kingdom as possible. To look at our social lives any other way is dangerous and ignorant of the larger picture. As Lionheart Warriors, we are always on duty and always on mission.

Knowing the stakes involved, let us influence those that influence us to His glory.

SECTION V
OUTER RING

CHAPTER 17
EXTEND THE TERRITORY

From the very beginning, God gave mankind certain duties and responsibilities that humans were particularly designed for. He gave us certain boundaries to have authority over. This was the original design for mankind. We were to be a caregiver over God's creation and property. We were to nurture, cultivate and care for the areas he assigned. Unfortunately, that authority was handed over to the enemy through rebellion and the disobedience of the fall.

During the rescue operation, we learned that Christ came to earth as the second official representative of mankind and took back authority handed over to the enemy. Jesus restored the ability for God's people to steward His creation. Unlike the original stewardship offered to Adam, this new stewardship is not without serious conflict. The restored stewardship is under constant attack by the enemy seeking to create havoc. There are definite holdover issues from the rebellion. These holdovers make it to where man's role is not quite as simple as it was prior to the fall.

There is now a built-in default within creation for chaos and turmoil. The creation is still fallen. Due to those repercussions, God's caregivers are not so singularly focused on their role as Adam was before. There is not only an ongoing battle from without, but one from within as well. Regardless, we must understand it is still the Lionheart Warrior's duty to fight, bring under control and maintain the particular areas of responsibility assigned by the King.

Our last area of operation is territorial. It is broken down into three battlefronts. They consist of calling, career and Kingdom expansion. The first two battlefronts, like all the ones prior, are unique to each individual. But the third is common to all warriors in the Kingdom. As we study and understand the first two battlefronts, we will begin seeing that our calling and careers create a launching point for influence outside of our relational and personal areas in this war.

These callings and careers are where we will make a fair share of our contact with those who exist outside our relational area. This can be both a positive and a negative. Our calling and career provide easy access to bring the Lionheart Warrior into areas not otherwise accessible for God's glory, but can also be a point at which the warrior can be faced with elements of personal failure and despair.

The enemy knows the power the first two battlefronts in this territorial AO have and it also knows how our jobs and finances have major influence over us. It knows most people define themselves by their jobs and judge their value based on the size of their paycheck. There is a disconnect when thinking about our jobs, finances and spiritual matters. For some reason, we tend to think they are not related. It is very easy to isolate our talents, calling and career areas of our existence to the purely material. If we do not keep these in the right spiritual perspective, our attitude can be a grave mistake that will cause turmoil in our path.

As an example, it is guaranteed any major criticism of Christianity in the past 50 years by its detractors has been brought about concerning the use and misuse of money (finance) and influence (calling). All major scandals involving the Church have had misuse of money or improper use of influence at their root. This is a common pitfall in all human endeavors. Spirituality is no different, but actually worse, all due to the connection to God in people's minds. The *Bible* has quite a bit to say on the subject of finances and how we, as Lionheart Warriors, handle our incomes. Management of our talents and treasures provides significant insight into the state of our spiritual life and therefore impacts the most important aspect of the territorial AO.

"For where your treasure is, there your heart will be also."
Matthew 6:21 NKJV

Out of all the battlefronts in this area of operation, expansion is by far the most important. All our efforts to this point are culminated here. The enemy's ultimate goal is to slow or stop this last battlefront from seeing any real success. Through direct or indirect attack, the enemy's ultimate focus is there. All the areas that precede expansion in our lives are in support of this fight.

As Lionheart Warriors, our role is ultimately toward this end and any attack we receive has this area as its true objective and target. In all honesty, this front is central to the whole Lionheart Warrior doctrine. Since the Kingdom expansion front is the last area we examine, it can be wrongly inferred it is the least of all the battlefronts. This cannot be farther from the truth—it is the whole goal.

As we learn to bring our areas of operation under the authority of our King, we are learning to refine and develop our ability to push this model out into the fallen world. The model was given to the original Lionheart Warriors, His disciples, during Christ's earthly life and it continues to this day through us.

Our role in the territorial AO is to identify and develop our unique talents and treasure given by God. The effects of this area have a residual effect on all the other areas and their respective battlefronts that preceded them. At the end of the day, we are dealing with people and, in dealing with people, we are dealing in relationships. That is the battleground for the war, and therefore our chief objective.

As those once superficial relationships develop and grow, their effects move closer and closer to the center rings of our areas of operation. We begin influencing more and getting influenced more. These individuals get closer and closer to our core being. How the warrior handles the territorial AO and the fruit produced there will cause a ripple effect that travels into our relational AO and even into our personal AO. Through God's grace and the use of His provided tools, we will achieve our objectives and bring glory to the King, all the while gaining more ground for His Kingdom.

To arms fellow warriors, it's time to push forward to victory.

CHAPTER 18
EQUIPPED TO WIN

We all have things we are naturally good at. All of us. At times, it can be difficult to fully understand what those things may be. Sometimes, we have a clear understanding of what they are and at other times, not so much. The things that we gravitate toward give us a good idea where we our calling in life might be. They are those certain areas we are passionate about that "speak" to us. We feel as though it is a fit or perfect match for our personality. We seem to be drawn to those areas and interests, almost like they are inherent within us. The concept of being "called" or in our "calling" can best be understood as that role in life that incorporates our purpose for being; that which makes us unique to everyone else; what we have been designed for.

One of the best ways to view one's calling is to get a sense of one's passions—those things that make our heart flutter—the thing that motivates us to reach higher. The Lord has created in each individual certain talents, gifts, bents and leanings. Let's face it, we are not all interested in the same things in life. Taking the necessary steps to learn and understand these promptings can go a long way to finding out where God would have us work in His Kingdom.

The area of calling can be a sore spot for some people. It can cause dread and apprehension due to not wanting to pursue the wrong path. They do not want to force the issue in a wrong direction. This is definitely true in cases where the inclination toward something is not very strong. They do not want to be passive when it's understood they should be going all in. Discovery of calling isn't as mystical as some imagine it. God is not a God of confusion. He desires for us to work in the purpose for which He made us. Unlike the fantasy movies, God rarely goes about calling His warriors through some sort of magical or esoteric means.

One of the greatest ways to have confidence in your spiritual walk as a Lionheart Warrior is to have a good understanding of the purpose God generally created for all mankind, that is to first and foremost be in fellowship with Him. God designed us to be in relationship. To be close to Him. For that reason, we were created above the animals.

Understanding and accepting this primary purpose keeps us focused and on the right path in life. We must begin and end from that purpose. Being connected to this makes it extremely difficult for the enemy to divert and distract us in the deeper journey for our specific purpose. Trials and tribulations come up in our journey, but all those work toward strengthening us in our discovery. Hardships and troubles push us closer to Him and strengthen our bond, which in turn, pushes us closer to our purpose. Launching from our fellowship with the Lord, we move toward revealing the use for our unique personalities and attributes in the furtherance of His Kingdom.

> *Hardships and troubles push us closer to Him and strengthen our bond, which in turn, pushes us closer to our purpose.*

"Trust in the LORD with all your heart, And lean not on your own understanding; In all your ways acknowledge Him, And He shall direct your paths."
Proverbs 3:5-6 NKJV

"Delight yourself also in the LORD, And He shall give you the desires of your heart. Commit your way to the LORD, Trust also in Him, And He shall bring it to pass."
Psalms 37:4-5 NKJV

With a desire for solid understanding of our unique role in the Kingdom, the Lionheart Warrior must work it out by the power given by the Spirit. In order to discover one's calling, it is vital to trust and rely on the Lord with all our heart. It is vital to find your heart's longing in Him. This is accomplished and worked out through prayer. Our heartfelt reliance on God's plan and purpose is exercised through sincere prayer. Wisdom is essential to the discovery process and God freely gives wisdom to those who sincerely request it. Our old "natural man" will attempt to influence and cause confusion in the area of our unique calling. This is another manifestation of the war between the flesh and Spirit. The flesh knows the stakes are high if the warrior is put in touch with their unique calling. Along with wisdom, the warrior must ask for discernment, discretion and diligence in this pursuit.

In order to trust in the Lord and not rely on our own understanding, we must not only be in constant prayer, but immersed in His word. God speaks and guides us through a small voice from within that is in agreement with His word. Seeking to be influenced by this "still small voice," we must make listening for it a part of our daily routine. To engage in the study of His word and being attentive to the promptings of His Spirit, is God's primary way of speaking to the warrior. It is through seeking His Kingdom first and foremost we will be led in truth. In an age where individuality and self-awareness are celebrated, the Lionheart Warrior must understand there is a trapping of self-centeredness and self-absorption inherent in pursuit of our calling.

In an attempt to mislead, the flesh will take every opportunity to divert and confuse the warrior as to our purpose. The enemy wants us to get lost in chasing our own tail. It wants us to spend time being self-absorbed and distracted from our focus on the things of God. The deception of self-fulfillment is so alluring and slippery. It has consumed millions of individuals with its trappings. The self-absorption trap dates back to the beginning of mankind and still plagues us today. All being born with a bias of self-absorption in our flesh, we are easily tempted by this selfish pursuit. The enemy knows we are tempted along these lines and counts on maximizing that leverage.

The Lionheart Warrior must know that any calling received will be along the path God designed and chose. God's choices are always motivated by His will and agenda for the Kingdom. His chief goal is for us to be an instrument for His glory, the glory found in the Son. All our bents, talents and passions He equips us with serve to further this agenda, the agenda of spreading the redemptive message of Jesus. God has chosen to be most glorified by the spreading of His Kingdom through this message.

Almighty God has chosen to redeem His people though the sacrificial life, death and resurrection of His Son. No matter what our talents or gifts may be, they will serve either directly or indirectly to spreading this message. For all the wonderful things we are capable of doing, this is our chief end and the very best use of our unique calling. No matter what role our call plays, all will find fulfillment in this conclusion.

God is a Father and His heart burns for His children. His plans are directed at saving and redeeming them. Any and all callings we receive from Him will have this objective as their central theme. We may be lawyers, doctors, artists or florists, but at the end of the day, we are agents engaged in the divine rescue business. We are all a part of the mission to rescue the lost. We are in the business of spreading the Word and snatching souls from eternal judgment.

At this point, the natural man within us speaks up. It becomes highly offended. The self-centered, me, me, me nature is appalled at this suggestion. It seeks to influence against this message. It wants to make our calling all about us and our own personal self-fulfillment, all about our particular journey in life. The flesh wants us to be shut off from this message. It wants us to examine alternate theories about God's calling on our lives. The flesh rationalizes there must be another reason for our calling.

Why is that? Why are we so hostile to the things to which God is so attracted?

The main reason our flesh doesn't want to bring people into God's Kingdom and favor is worship. The natural man hates worshiping God. It wants worship all for itself. It hates serving God. It wants devotion and service directed toward itself. Our flesh wants all of our intentions and thoughts in life to revolve around self. The flesh is a false god that longs for everything to center on it. Worship of God or the worship of self? Answering the call of purpose in the warrior's life is ultimately answering the call to worship. How will we be used and to what end?

> *"For I know the plans I have for you," declares the Lord,*
> *"plans to prosper you and not to harm you, plans to give*
> *you hope and a future."*
> *Jeremiah 29:11 NIV*

The Creator designed His creation for particular tasks and purposes. His plans and purposes were hatched before there ever was a creation. All was brought forth to accomplish His will. Any and all our talents, gifts, opportunities and objectives are to that end and that end only. The enemy wants to subvert that. The Lionheart Warrior must fight to keep things on track. We must look to and constantly lean on the Lord's directions and ways. We must rely on the power and wisdom given by the Holy Spirit.

> *"I, therefore, the prisoner of the Lord, beseech you to walk*
> *worthy of the calling with which you were called, with all*
> *lowliness and gentleness, with longsuffering, bearing with*
> *one another in love, endeavoring to keep the unity of the*
> *Spirit in the bond of peace."*
> *Ephesians 4:1-3 NKJV*

We must be diligent in the application of all that this requires by His word. In following this, we find the key to understanding the strategy of our calling as laid out by the Lord. Through the unity with the Lord and unity with others in the building of God's Kingdom, we will work out His unique calling on our lives. All this by knowing the Lord wills for us to walk in that calling with Him. For He is most glorified there.

Let us therefore use our calling to push forward in the purposes for which we were made.

CHAPTER 19
FOCUSED EFFORT

It never fails, take any two people who do not know each other, throw them in a room, and within minutes they will be talking about their work. It is unavoidable. We have a tendency to define ourselves by what we do for a living. We cannot avoid thinking of defining ourselves by not necessarily who we are, but what we do for money. Ask a child what they want to be when they grow up and you will get a laundry list of occupations such as fireman, policeman, soldier, doctor, etc. Let's face it, if we are not gainfully employed, most of our self-images would be in shambles.

We find it hard to feel good about our state in life if we are jobless. To that point, the number one stressor of men 25 to 50 years of age is job related. It is hard to avoid this fact; we find our identity in our work. We are working beings. If you go all the way back to the beginning, the Creator placed the first man in a position of authority and gave him a job to do.

> "Then the LORD God took the man and put him in the
> garden of Eden to tend and keep it."
> Genesis 2:15 NKJV

He was given two major roles, to "tend" the garden and to "keep" the garden. Adam was to take charge, nurture and grow the garden he was given. He was tasked with protecting and serving it. The first man was given command of the Lord's property. At the time, he had the most important job in all the earth — and he blew it.

As a ramification for his failure on the job, the job he once knew as a source of wonder and worship, turned into a source of pain and struggle. After the fall, God revealed the consequences of his sinful actions. According to the curse handed down, the man would now see his work in a different light. After the fall, Adam's view of God, view of self, view of his wife and now his view of work all changed. He was going to know and experience hardship to get the same results he once had without said hardship. This would encapsulate all his efforts going forward. Everything now carried varying levels of difficulty.

The nature of the fallen world dictates life is going to be a hard and uphill battle. There will be trauma associated with feeding ourselves (earning a wage) and there will be setbacks. We will definitely experience let downs and frustrations. It is the nature of things. Despite the fact of these truths, there is hope and we do not need to lead lives of desperation in our work. There is a better way, a way that transcends this fallen world.

We are convinced our effort is for the greater cause. Our motivations for going to work are not just to climb a corporate ladder or attempt to please our boss, but for a more fulfilling cause.

The divine rescue operation provided the way. The King redeemed our work. He re-established our joy in all things. He restored our view of work to its original design. As a result, the Lionheart Warrior understands daily work is for a greater purpose than simply "feeding ourselves." We understand our work is for something higher than earning a wage. We are convinced our effort is for the greater cause. Our motivations for going to work are not just to climb a corporate ladder or attempt to please our boss, but for a more fulfilling cause.

"Whether you eat or drink or whatever you do, do all to
the Glory of God"
1 Corinthians 10:31 NKJV

This verse is often overlooked and mostly gets confined to food and drink choices. The meaning of this verse carries a much higher truth with serious weight for us as warriors. It speaks to our ultimate motivation in all of our efforts in life. It goes to the heart of our intentions in our actions. This command from God is not to be restricted to eating, but is to be a mission statement for all our efforts. This verse is to be our mantra. As we go about our day-to-day tasks, this concept of making it a form of worship should guide our every thought. Grasping this concept, we realize we are to work as if the Lord is our boss. All our motivations, intentions and efforts are to define us as warriors set apart for God. Our attitude toward work has a supernatural relevance. Our efforts speak to a higher purpose beyond this natural world.

Since the fall of man and the curse inflicted on Adam, we have struggled with defining ourselves by our work. It haunts us in more ways than we care to examine. Why else when we meet a person for the first time do we feel inclined to bring up work and compare stories? We naturally make assessments based on the other person's occupation. We make conscious and unconscious judgments based on their chosen career fields. As humans, we are bent toward this. We feel a person's chosen field tells us all we need to know about them.

When introducing ourselves, we instinctively start by what we do for a living. If it is not the first thing we discuss, it will definitely be next on the list. Is it any wonder why it is so personally devastating to people when they get laid off from a job? Talk about an attack on one's self-image. We might as well be branded a loser and considered a drag on society, when jobless.

Through ongoing conditioning, the world system pushes us to define ourselves by the jobs we hold. We are viewed as workers. We are viewed as laborers and if the role is not a lofty or prestigious one, we suffer an internal war of frustration, doubt and insignificance. We are a product of the Adamic curse. And if you do not think the enemy doesn't attack through this mindset, you are being delusional.

In order to avoid these trappings, it is vital we understand this concept and be on the lookout for it. We must recognize and understand how the enemy uses these beliefs to keep us powerless in the workplace. Fearing the loss of our job, the enemy will sow doubt concerning our true calling. It will use this fear of loss to stifle and hamstring us. This is how the enemy keeps us from following the call to God's glory in our careers. Wanting to side track us, the enemy fuels this internal conflict created by our insecurities. We will hold back for fear of retaliation from our employers.

> *"And whatever you do, do it heartily, as to the Lord and not to men, knowing that from the Lord you will receive the reward of the inheritance; for you serve the Lord Christ."*
> Colossians 3:23-24 NKJV

God places his warriors in areas of influence all around the world. He uses these individuals to carry out His mandate and will. The Lionheart Warrior is sensitive to this call in life, and looks for every opportunity to represent his King. While working toward the goals the King lays on our hearts, it is important to stay plugged into His truth. It is vital to stay connected to the source of our power. To accomplish a divine sync with the King's promptings, we must meet with and remain in constant daily contact with Him. We must make this interaction our priority through prayer and study of His Word.

The warrior is an ambassador for the Kingdom and our actions reflect that. Being a representative is not a burden to be endured, but an honor and divine privilege bestowed. If we see it as a daunting and burdensome task, we will look for options and excuses to avoid the Lord's promptings. We are called to delight in His labors. God provides the grace and the joy needed to influence and impact others for His kingdom. The Lionheart Warrior accepts that challenge daily. We live and love to reflect positively on the King and on His Kingdom.

In an effort to understand our mission, we must grasp a major part of the King's desire for us to serve our fellow co-workers. We not only perform our assigned work, but look to be a service to others at work. We are called to have a heart for them in all areas of life. We are in the King's service and He requires we pass His love on to the others within our reach.

Understand that most of God's promptings have to do with serving other people. God's heart burns for His people and spreading the good news of His redemption and provision. He is glorified by those who trust and rely on Him. Ultimately, we are in the game of seeking out those who are wayward and pouring the King's love on them. In our daily tasks, we will be provided opportunities to step in and provide necessary words or deeds that will make an eternal impact. There are lost, hurting and struggling people everywhere and we are to notice, locate and intervene when possible. These are people we know and people we do not know; people we like and people we may not like. If we want to be respected, then we respect them. If we want to be appreciated, then we appreciate them. If we want to be utilized, then we utilize them. Keep in mind, this command is even more true for our fellow brothers and sisters in the faith.

Jesus taught us we are defined by our love for one another. Extra steps are to be taken for our brothers and sisters in the Kingdom. We are required to take care of our own. They are our family. This requires us to treat others exactly how we would want them to treat us. This is our true calling. This is our fight.

Bottom line, God is looking to bring more Lionheart Warriors into the fold. He is about expanding the rescue operation to all those still lost and without Him. At times, we are to be reckless in our rescue attempts for others. We know the stakes are high. Our King showed us the way. Jesus provided us an illustration of His radical love for the desperate and hurting. He lived the example of a shepherd who leaves His flock to go out and rescue the lost and wayward one. He believes the risk is well worth it and so do we. The lost are everywhere. As those without Him, they are under constant attack. They experience setbacks and failures. They need what we have been given. This is His work. This is our work. This is the true fight.

Therefore, it's time to get to work.

CHAPTER 20

GAINING GROUND

"If you are not growing, you are dying."

We often here that statement as it pertains to business. I have also heard it applied to overall personal development. If you are not actively trying to improve and discover new territory in business, your competition certainly is. Our last area of operation has a similar philosophy, but with a slight twist. When it comes to spiritual matters, it may read better like this:

"If we are not growing, then they are dying."

Hopefully, we have established that the stakes are high in this war. We have not been discussing one of many available philosophical options in life. For the follower of Christ, this is the only option. People are lost and hurting and our King commands we go find them.

If we are not expanding His kingdom, then they are dying.

Our last battlefront as Lionheart Warriors is the culmination of all our talents, skills, strategies and efforts in this life. It is the reason you have purpose, significance and design. Fundamentally, it is the expansion of God's Kingdom. It is the multiplication and duplication of His army. Quite simply, it all boils down to taking new spiritual territory, expanding the Lord's Kingdom footprint. Taking back His creation. As Lionheart Warriors, we are the extension of His grace sent out into this fallen world. We are to push forward as a unit with the goal of reaching the ends of the earth. God is redeeming His people through one Lionheart Warrior at a time.

Jesus came to earth to establish the Kingdom of God, a kingdom unlike one ever conceived before. With that goal in mind, He took on our humanity and paid our spiritual debt of sin. He bore our spiritual punishment, so we did not have to. All this was done to satisfy the holiness of God, while at the same time expressing His heart for mercy. The perfect sacrifice. The perfect gift. Redeeming us out of slavery. By setting everything right, He guaranteed justice for our crimes while simultaneously, broking us free from the weight of eternal punishment. Through His actions on the battlefield, He provided the path for peace to enter back into eternal fellowship with Himself. Once realized, God's people could live in connection and communion with their glorious King and one another. Relationship between the Sovereign and His people was reestablished, restored and made new.

Unlike in the garden before the fall, we live in hostile territory. We are under constant threat. The world system we once trusted is in cahoots with our enemy. We are surrounded on all sides by those who are still in open rebellion against the King and outright hostile toward His agenda. Our new community is under constant barrage from those forces and we must utilize all the tools provided to combat them. Having been empowered through prayer, study of God's word and fellowship with other believers, we have all the necessary resources to fight the good fight.

We as Lionheart Warriors were not tasked with maintaining our own personal victories, but joining other Lionheart Warriors in their fight.

We as Lionheart Warriors were not tasked with maintaining our own personal victories, but joining other Lionheart Warriors in their fight. Together having been designated with spreading the truth of God's plan, we are to seek out those opposing forces in league with the enemy. We are tasked with entering in to spiritual battles with them and push back against the larger enemy.

> *"For we do not wrestle against flesh and blood, but against*
> *principalities, against powers, against the rulers of the*
> *darkness of this age, against spiritual hosts of wickedness*
> *in the heavenly places."*
> *Ephesians 6:12 NKJV*

The Kingdom is expanded through the liberation of the soul of individuals by sharing the life-giving good news of God's Son. With utmost reliance on God, the good news is presented to those still hostile. All this with the hope God will work in their heart to receive it with trusting faith. While believing and trusting in the Lord, the message is delivered by warriors with the expectation that lost souls will believe and receive it. It should be noted here; as a word of caution, we warriors still fight internal battles of pride and arrogance. Therefore, we can get confused into thinking our clever presentation of the good news is what leads to others receptiveness. We must guard against spiritual arrogance and the influence of our flesh in wanting to take credit. Remember, only by the power of God do their eyes become open and receive.

As a sold-out child of God, we should definitely experience joy from doing our King's bidding, as long as we remember not to become cocky. In our former fallen state, we had tendencies to take credit for good things we did not do. That nature is still present and must be kept in check. By the power the King provides, we will do just that. As laid out plainly in God's word, the prompting of His Spirit is the deciding factor in the believing process and we are merely servants of the message. We have been favored to partner with the Lord in this supernatural process. We are to be diligent soldiers on mission, fully prepared to be used at a moment's notice.

The Lionheart Warrior does have a major role in preparation and diligence of delivering the good news. We have to be utterly familiar with His saving message. Having ourselves been freed from bondage, we have an obligation to share our own personal story of redemption and how exactly the Lord moved in our life. We must be in constant prayer on behalf of those individuals the Lord places before us. With an attitude of trust and reliance on the Spirit, He will prompt and guide the warrior toward those individuals who are ready and willing to heed the call. Through direction from the Lord, the warrior will set out to accomplish what was placed on our heart.

Once we deliver His message, we are required to assist with any spiritual questions or points of clarity the person may have. There will be a loving willingness on our part to assist that person coming to believe and trust the message we delivered. It is at this point the enemy will come out to combat the receiving of the lifesaving information. The individual's fleshly nature will come out against the truth. Occasionally, there will be times some of the hearers will respond with hostility.

We must not forget, the Lord's redemptive message is a direct attack on the fallen nature of the hearer. Despite the strong temptation to respond in kind, the warrior must not take it personal, stay calm and remain focused on the mission. Never lose sight that our fleshly nature would love the opportunity to react to any negativities presented from the hearer with hostilities of its own. We, as warriors, are mandated to represent the Kingdom rightly by not taking it personally. We are to maintain the same spirit as our Lord modeled when He was insulted and attacked delivering the truth at His trial.

Make no mistake, the enemy is formidable and will come out hard against these rescue missions. Resistance will manifest in all kinds of different ways with the ultimate goal of confusion, stifling or out right ceasing of Kingdom efforts. Since this is a spiritual issue, part of the preparation for expansion missions is to saturate ourselves in prayer and the putting on of God's armor. There is no shortcut to this end.

We are on a spiritual mission and therefore we need serious spiritual preparation.

Through the use of strong spiritual discipline, we place emphasis on reliance and trust in the Almighty, recognizing He is in control and directs our every step. In doing this, we keep the right attitude of humility for our mission. We are reminded the victory belongs to the Lord and we must look to Him to move it forward. Our attitude spurs a right perspective concerning the seriousness of our mission and the King's methods for its development.

By staying saturated in His word and in constant communication with Him, we remain fully prepared mentally and spiritually to enter into these hostile environments. Having the Lord's battle plan in place will make it rather difficult for the enemy to catch us by surprise. We will not lose focus while engaged in going after the lost and enslaved. By maintaining the mindset, we are wholly reliant on the power of the Lord both in this action and resolve. He works in and through us to accomplish these objectives. We are but willing participants in His rescue operations. He has made this His priority.

Battlefront expansion is not secondary to the other areas in our lives. If anything, our other areas are all but a preparation for the expansion battlefront. Both our personal and relational AOs are an extension of the King's expansive agenda. Overall, we are a part of His movement to create a community living in Kingdom fellowship with one another. Through the process of expansion, we will witness the divine process of those we are attempting to reach, slowly transition into our other areas.

These new Kingdom recruits will start moving closer to our middle ring, while others will remain in our calling and career areas. This is a natural occurrence of Kingdom fellowship. Through the seasons of life, some people get closer to us than others. This occurs as the warrior connects and lives life in fellowship with those rescued to the Kingdom.

We are ever bringing those who were far away, closer and closer to the core of our mission. The overall mission converts into a divine multiplication process. The Lord's Kingdom is about building a dynamic family unit, a warrior clan. The once strange and potentially hostile individual becomes a kindred sibling in Christ. Being guided and taught to become Lionheart Warriors, they will be trained up and sent on mission, just like we were which came before them. It is a process of duplication and a force multiplier. A chain of events constantly expanding the Kingdom and developing powerful warriors to drive forward and conquer. We are ever to be pushing farther and deeper into the enemy's strong hold.

As primary objective and chief operational goal, Lionheart Warriors are always about the expansion mission. When it comes down to it, the King has set us free to then go forth and set others free. We accomplish this through the ways and means He established. We are steadfast in securing and strengthening our personal, relational and territorial AOs, while fully focused on battlefront expansion. Everything is a work up toward this end. While there is still breath in our lungs, we as Lionheart Warriors are committed to rescuing just one more fallen soul for the King. All other objectives pale in comparison or at least act as waypoints toward this end.

For King and Kingdom.

Section VI
Get in the Fight

CHAPTER 21
BATTLE PLAN

"And let us not grow weary while doing good, for in due season we shall reap if we do not lose heart."
Galatians 6:9 NKJV

As we bring our study of the Lionheart Warrior to a close, we need to dive into the application of these truths. We need to have a way to put these principles to use immediately. We have examined the reasons for the war, the enemy, the tools and the areas we must take charge over. Knowing that the enemy is already at work in our areas of responsibility, there must be steps taken to systematically counter it. We have the necessary knowledge to move forward, but there are still a few concepts missing that need to be discussed. We are in need of a game plan to put all this knowledge into practice in our daily lives. In order to experience victory, we must be doers of these truths and not just knowers of them. God has established and supplied all we need to proceed forward in His power and confidence.

In the next few chapters, we will discuss how to take the concepts we learned and put them into our daily routine. Starting with the first part of our day and moving to the end of our day, we desperately need direction and guidance from our King. Just like military units who go out on mission, we must receive orders, formulate specific strategies and set objectives prior to heading out. This is vital, otherwise, we will find ourselves trying to manage utter chaos in our battlefronts. The enemy counts on us being utterly wrapped in chaos.

As Lionheart Warriors, we have ways to examine our daily actions for progress and potential mistakes. We must be guided in our assessment of the results and how to make proper adjustments in line with God's purposes. Additionally, we need ways to get back on track when things do not go according to plan. In the spirit of lessons learned on the battlefield, we as warriors must have a way to recover and recuperate from the stresses of battle by way of "licking our wounds." During our fights with the enemy, we are sure to face stiff resistance in our Areas of Operation that will definitely come at a cost. We personally do not have all the answers to the problems that are guaranteed to come our way, therefore, we will need help and counsel along the way.

While moving from one operation to another, it is imperative to have support and assistance from other warriors and units. More often than not, we will need to join forces with these other warriors in pursuit of common objectives. Especially in the area of Kingdom expansion, we will be called to coordinate efforts with other Lionheart Warriors by our King. We must strive to create teams of warriors who join together to do battle with the enemy. We must locate and nurture those edifying and encouraging relationships. It is through unity, we will see serious progress in the field and be able to stand up to all the assaults.

Lastly, we will need to understand how to sustain a prolonged fight in our battlefronts. As warriors, we are on the time line of our King. We stay on the frontlines until He calls us home. We may be on this mission and in this fight for many years, therefore we need to take the time to understand long term strategy for pushing forward as His warriors.

As we hit the home stretch, let us stay focused on our true mission and intentions. Let us not get wrapped up in the potential of all of this, but truly take the time to form our lives around this strategy and its implementation. Do not let this become just another book in a long line of works that make us feel inspired while we are reading it, only for the motivation to fade as the last page gets turned. Push forward my fellow warriors, the beginning is in sight and we have been given ultimate victory.

BATTLE PLAN

Time to strap up and strap in, our Lion roars.

CHAPTER 22
KING'S BRIEF

"What are your orders, Commander?"

Where do we go from here? Is this all theoretical or are there certain steps that can be taken in order to see progress, establish goals and see results in this war? One of the biggest complaints about this particular subject is the emphasis on the concepts, but little in the way of application. As a warrior, we want to know we are making progress. We want to see the mistakes made and the areas in which we need to make adjustments. The *Bible* is very clear that the wise man loves correction and instruction, always seeking self-improvement.

The ability to fight a physical war in the natural sense definitely requires a physically fit warrior. The individual must be highly-trained in order to endure the rigors of combat. They must be able to use strength, endurance and power in taking the fight to the enemy. That requires a tremendous amount of attention and effort in the realm of physical training.

Unlike the conventional warrior, the Lionheart Warrior does not have many physical training requirements. Ours are necessary spiritual and mental requirements in order to pursue combat readiness. Do not be mistaken, our readiness to fight requires endurance, strength and power as well, but on a whole nother level. We must be strong in the Lord and the power of His might in order to put up a good fight. That requires daily, if not moment-by-moment, connection to our commander. Our fight demands constant instruction and direction. We war against powers not of this world, therefore, we need connection not of this world. We need to go before our mighty King and receive His powerful all sufficient grace daily.

Every good military commander has a process to issue orders to his troops and make battlefield adjustments during combat. There must be clear lines of communication and a clear path to accomplish objectives or there will be a detrimental loss of morale. Loss of morale can seriously hamper any high-level unit's ability for mission readiness. The Lionheart Warrior's battles are no exception. We too must receive instruction and correction daily. Our commander needs to make adjustments to our actions and intents constantly.

Before embarking on any mission, a commanding officer will call a meeting to discuss the mission objectives with his unit leaders. He will lay out his goals and objectives and make sure to emphasize the particular importance of each one. By doing that, he insures that everyone is on the same page and working toward the same objective. This meeting will also help prevent overlap and potential friendly fire scenarios. Cohesion is assured and it provides a way for both command and troops to stay connected. This meeting time is referred to as a mission brief. A King's Brief.

In the military, mission briefs can be designated as "all hands on deck", this means every person with any connection or duty to the mission is required to attend. In these "all hands" briefs, vital information is disseminated that cannot be lost through the chain of command, therefore all necessary parties need to be in attendance.

Our commander has designated His King's briefs that way. Attendance is vital to all Lionheart Warriors. During His briefs, objectives are laid out and, inside those objectives, detailed tasks need to be accomplished. Tasks and objectives are added, removed or altered depending on the need of the mission. Basically, we need to be adaptive in order to be effective in our duty. We must know our role back and forth, left and right, up and down. King's briefs are mission critical.

For the mission of the Lionheart Warrior, we have been assigned roles and duties for which God has specifically designed us. We have a specific mission in specific areas of the Kingdom. We know how important they are to the overall mission of God's Kingdom agenda. We understand we have an enemy who is intelligent and formidable. We understand this enemy will stop at nothing to undermine the cause. We understand the stakes are high, therefore our preparation to meet those demands must also be high.

Military commanders hold mission briefs prior to sending their troops out into the field. Our King has the same policy. Looking at the life of Jesus, our perfect example of a spiritual warrior on mission, we see while on earth He took the time to separate Himself and commune with His heavenly Father. He separated Himself away from distractions and competing voices in order to communicate effectively. While engaged in the divine rescue operation, it appears Jesus did this prior to every big mission. He separated Himself before the day began, to be alone with the Father, get those last-minute instructions and a morale boost prior to stepping out into battle. In doing that, He provided the perfect example and demonstrated the value He placed upon the daily King's brief. We are to follow suit. If the perfect Son of God found King's Briefs important, so should those who go out and fight in His name.

Daily task orders are critical in meeting assigned objectives. It provides opportunity to focus, get clarity and boost morale prior to us stepping off. Our spirit is rejuvenated. Our mind gets focused and our body awakens to God's plans and purposes for the day. We must take the time to separate ourselves in preparation for the battles ahead.

As a practical concept, below is an example of how it can be incorporated:

If the Lionheart Warrior is set to leave the house to start their daily schedule at 7 a.m., then they need to wake up at least 1.5 hours prior. Barring any other factors, this time provides a sufficient period to not only get prepared to leave in the natural (brush teeth, shower, get dressed, eat, etc.), but also go before the King. They can take each of their areas of operation before the King and discuss them. In doing that, they can request insight and provision to combat the potential issues each area may hold.

> *We must partner with God who is for us and rely on His ways and means to accomplish our tasks as laid out in His word. One major way that is accomplished is through prayer.*

The *Bible* makes a clear distinction that we should walk according to the Spirit and not according to the flesh. We must partner with God who is for us and rely on His ways and means to accomplish our tasks as laid out in His word. One major way that is accomplished is through prayer. Our link to the spiritual is through faith in God by the exercise of prayer. Through prayer the Lionheart Warrior reaches out to the supernatural. We connect to our true source of power. A simple example of prayer can look like the following:

"Heavenly Father, thank you for the opportunity to come before you this morning to receive my instructions and fellowship for the day. I know you have a plan and a purpose for me to follow today. I ask that you guide and lead me as I go about my tasks and let me be always mindful of your agenda and not my own. I ask for your power as I worship, read your word and pray for the areas of my life. All glory to you in the name of your Son Jesus, Amen."

After prayer, you can either sing a praise and worship song you pre-selected or move right into reading of God's word. I personally read five chapters from the book of Psalms and one chapter from the book of Proverbs every morning. There are other times, I will work through the Gospels or epistles reading one or more chapters a day. The daily reading sets the tone for my day and gets me focused on Kingdom things. The point is to read and meditate on God's word, receiving His instruction and guidance on all matters.

The text must always be read in context and received in the spirit and intent it was originally written. Keep in mind, our flesh will always look to distort God's word to fit its agenda. Prayerfully, we must seek and receive the truth even if it challenges our sensibilities and biases.

As a gentle word of caution: Do not forget one of the enemies we face is our fleshly fallen nature. Our old man will be offended and attempt to twist and distort God's truth to make it more acceptable. By relying on the power of the Spirit, this enemy will be defeated in this area. The enemy will eventually give up trying to distort the Word and will shift to try and confuse us on that particular truth's application. The enemy is crafty and this twisting of the truth is a perfect example of the battlefront of the mind.

Given the gravity of the resistance and the stakes of our mission, the daily King's briefs are crucial to our success. Do not be frustrated; this is a lifelong battle and it will take some time and effort to get better at fighting it. Reliance on the power of the Holy Spirit will see us through, it is He who teaches and leads the way.

Through regular daily commitment of time and attention to meeting with God, we will receive supernatural guidance in our life. It is to be done with a confident expectation that God wills our understanding and wants us to connect to Him in meaningful ways. Making this time one of the most valuable parts of our daily schedules is a must in order to perceive any progress and success in our lives.

As we spend quality time getting to know the King and His mission for our day, we as warriors will experience the power He reveals and the abundant life He promises. As we stay consistent in this, insight will be gained in our three major areas of operation (personal, relational and territorial) and adjustments will be made to counter enemy activity there. The Lord will empower us to stand firm against the enemy and be able to taste the victory He has already so richly provided.

Let us go before Him, that we may joyfully receive our orders.

CHAPTER 23
AFTER THE ACTION

Once military units return from accomplishing their mission, they need to decompress and give an account of the operation to their superiors. After offloading their gear and downloading their weapons, those leaders in charge will go before their commander for what is referred to as an AAR. AAR is a military acronym that stands for "After Action Report."

In military operations, the AAR is a vital leadership tool used by commanders to access, document, discuss and analyze events both positive and negative that occurred during the mission. These meetings require high levels of honesty and personal accountability. During the reporting process, the commander is first provided all the his leader's opinions and perspectives of what occurred during the mission. Once those leaders explain actions taken, the commander will then ask follow up probing questions. This style of questioning provides the commander an opportunity to best understand how things transpired during the mission and ultimately if it was a success or not.

There are many vital reasons for conducting AARs, but one of the most beneficial to the individual warrior is learning what they can do differently next time. In these debriefs, warriors are shown the necessary corrections to ensure success in future missions. It provides an opportunity for "lessons learned."

Just like in those military operations, our King wants a detailed AAR with His courageous Lionheart Warriors. He wants us to go over our daily operations and for us to give a thorough account. During our King's debrief, we get to express how we thought things went. Unlike the human military commanders, our God is all-knowing and there is nothing that surprises Him. He already knows whether we are going to be 100-percent truthful in our assessment or not. He knows all the "lessons learned" before the initial actions were even taken. He desires to be in fellowship with us and for us to long to be in fellowship with Him. The AAR is not for Him per se, but for us. Our King knows we need to share our victories and defeats with Him, because we need the connection. He knows we need to get things off our chests, especially when things go wrong. He designed us that way.

> *It is a time for the Lionheart Warrior to look back on the day and be exposed to insights the Spirit delivers from searching our hearts.*

Our King's debrief is a special time of prayer and reflection. It is a time for the Lionheart Warrior to look back on the day and be exposed to insights the Spirit delivers from searching our hearts. We need this time of introspection to keep our life in the right perspective. As sinful humans, we have a tendency to fall back into self-sufficiency and sinful pride. As we take the time to give account of our day's activities, we are taking the subordinate role in this divine relationship. This subordinate role keeps us humble and focused on our proper place within the Kingdom. We reacknowledge His authority and our submission to that authority.

It is during the spiritual AAR with our King, we have an opportunity to offer up praise, worship and thanksgiving. We acknowledge not only what transpired during our time on mission, but also give thanks for the amazing opportunities afforded us. We recognize and express gratitude for the blessings of God being worked out in us and through us.

"I will praise You, O LORD, with my whole heart; I will tell of all Your marvelous works."
-Psalm 9:1 NKJV

The reflective nature of this meeting with the King provides the perfect opportunity to confess any shortcomings we had during our day. Like all warriors engaged in warfare, there is a certain element of mishaps and mistakes that are made. Having the best intentions in mind, we make poor choices. We make wrong decisions. We revert back to the flesh as opposed to the Spirit in our actions. At times, we may have acted out of selfish desire instead of humble service. We have a King who understands us. We have a God who knows all things and has forgiveness waiting. In His divine understanding, He has taken all issues into account beforehand.

> *"If we say that we have no sin, we deceive ourselves, and the truth is not in us. If we confess our sins, He is faithful and just to forgive us our sins and to cleanse us from all unrighteousness"–1 John 1:9 KJV*

LESSONS LEARNED

Through Christ, we have the forgiveness we need to cover all our mistakes. We have the cleansing we need to be at peace with our calling. We are finite creatures, mistakes will be made and we will fall short, but God has provided the way. We only have to admit them, turn from them and receive His grace.

The weight of unconfessed and unrepentant sin will severely hamper our connection with the Lord. It will cause us to block blessings we most desperately need. During further fighting, we will remain weak and vulnerable. Through confession, repentance and forgiveness, we will be healed and brought back into proper fellowship with the King.

In our King's debrief, we have access to a loving God who provides us an opportunity to express our wants and needs. This designated time of reflecting on the past mission spurs in us a true sense and understanding of all our needs. As we reflect on our past day's actions, both good and bad, we cannot help but think about what lies ahead of us tomorrow. We see out into the next day's operations and beyond.

It is at this time, we need to understand that any grace we are given from the Lord is for the present only. He provides for our needs within the short range. Throughout His word there are countless examples of His people wanting provision for the long term. They wanted provision for their future endeavors. They wanted security that would allow them to rely on themselves and their understanding of things, rather than God. Story after story provides evidence He does not operate this way. He only provides for the present. As our sovereign Lord, He wants us to be in constant fellowship and reliance on Him. Trusting in His strength and learning not to trust in our own.

In addition, there will be situations where we need to request assistance with things that were left undone in our immediate or even distant past—situations we have either ignored or long forgotten. As we get into a mode of reflecting, those old situations have a tendency to pop back up—situations that had to be pushed off to the next day, perhaps even well beyond that—situations in which we do not still have influence, but require supernatural attention. Amazingly, we have a King who is in control and can be trusted to engage with and take care of all things. He is a God from which nothing can escape. He is a God who is in utter control. Gracefully, we can boldly go before Him in all these situations and circumstances while knowing full well He is listening.

"Let us therefore come boldly to the throne of grace, that we may obtain mercy and find grace to help in time of need."
Hebrews 4:16 NKJV

As we can see, Lionheart Warriors have the privilege of going to the King before the mission, during the mission and after mission to get what is needed. We do not have a commander who is detached from His troops. We do not have a leader too busy with the activities of other units who cannot be bothered with ours. We have a King who longs to teach us how to correct our mistakes. We have a King who wants to share in our victories. We have a King who supports us.

It is through taking the time to bring ourselves and our daily operations before Him that we can experience the full benefit of His provision and power for us. The King's debrief is just as vital as the King's brief early in the morning. In it we have opportunity to receive healing, cleansing and a renewed sense of purpose. Thankfully, we will be fully recharged and recuperated, so when we go back out on mission, we will be stronger than before. Our King has set up the ultimate process to accomplish missions for His kingdom. He has set up not only a system for us to be taught by Him, but also one where we can receive follow-up support and necessary course corrections. He has established an even greater support network in which we can join with other Lionheart Warriors on their journey.

By divine strategy, we are not only in our personal fight, but linked with others in their fight. Our King has set up a buddy system. He has created a process to receive back up and support. In His word, He demands we work closely with other warriors in this war. He has provided us with kindred soldiers who will assist in our weaknesses and lift us up in our strengths.

Thankfully, we are not lone operators in this conflict, but bound together in the same cause, under the same banner and King. Let us take the opportunity to double our efforts and strength by partnering and joining in fellowship with those called together by God. By the counsel of His perfect will, let us learn to link up and connect with the other warriors He has placed in our path. In doing this, we will leave a lasting impact for the Kingdom we could not have done otherwise. For we are united toward His Kingdom and His glory.

Warriors Unite!

CHAPTER 24
COMBINING FORCES

S ince the dawn of mankind, all the warriors who ever existed have been a part of a unit. They have operated and been supported by brothers in arms who shared common goals, common training and common experiences. These units formed a bond and an identity that carried them through some of the most horrific situations known to man. These warrior units protected each other, strengthened each other, challenged each other and pushed each other to be the very best they could be. They became something bigger than themselves.

> *"As iron sharpens iron, so a man sharpens the countenance of his friend."*
> *Proverbs 27:17 NKJV*

This verse is used in all kinds of different scenarios from *Bible* studies to flag football tournaments. The concept is pretty sound. In order for iron to obtain a razor's edge and be formed into a weapon of warfare, it must be scraped violently against another piece of iron. The two pieces of iron spark and flash. Friction is created. All the rough edges get chipped away, until both pieces develop that razor-sharp edge.

This metaphor points to a refining and crafting process found throughout God's word. The Creator designed His people to be in fellowship with one another. That fellowship is not confined to potluck lunches and handshakes every Sunday. He desires for them to challenge, encourage, empower and sharpen each other. They are to fight side by side.

The sharpening process is critical to fighting this war. We are called to take the fight to God's enemies—a fight beyond our visual world. In order to prevail, we are going to need the support and accountability that can only come through strong bonds of brotherhood. Brotherhood is vital to warriorhood. The Lionheart Warrior needs to be connected to fellow fighters in kind. We need constant training and accountability. The stresses of fighting on the battlefronts of our lives will wear each of us down. It will cause us to stumble and fall. It will diminish our morale and weaken our resolve.

The Lionheart Warrior must operate in community. We must align ourselves in a group who will build us up, a group that challenges actions and motivations, a group that gives us counsel and goes to war with us in prayer. We were redeemed to operate in a group of like-minded warriors to encourage, support and strengthen each other. The process of supporting each other in the team has a rebounding effect. What we put out to others, returns back to us in compounded ways. God designed us that way. As we pour out our support and service to others, it returns back to us magnified. It is a supernatural occurrence that is built into God's process and cannot be avoided. We are to embrace it and harness its power, pushing the unit of Lionheart Warriors toward victory.

Even though we as humans are naturally drawn toward groups of like-interest, we tend to avoid openness and shun support. In our flesh, we do not like to look weak and vulnerable. Our flesh prompts us to project strength and competency at all times. The World System has convinced us that getting involved with others in supporting fellowship is soft, effeminate and not warrior-like. We make up excuses why not to get involved. We cover up for the pride found in feelings of inadequacy and insecurity. We prefer not to get involved in order to avoid exposure. We convince ourselves that we do not need to be in fellowship with others. We get sold on the idea we have everything we need. We rationalize that any course of action contrary to sufficiency within ourselves confirms a deep-seated fear that we are an imposter.

Our enemy is a liar.

The enemy wants us isolated, alone and cut off. The enemy wants us unsupported and self-sufficient, making it easier to surround us, to outnumber us and to cut us off from our backup. The enemy wants the warrior trapped in the echo chamber of their mind.

As a police officer, I was taught to always request backup even in some of the most mundane calls for service. The mantra, "Don't be the hero," was always preached. We were taught that it was vital to get another set of eyes on the situation. This created a force multiplier in the mind of the enemy. There is strength in numbers. There is power in community. Ambush is easier when the targets are few. The enemy is a bully. They want all the odds in their favor. They need us to go at them alone. For alone, we are an easy target and when we are all by ourselves, the enemy knows it has the best shot at defeating us.

> *"For where two or three are gathered together in My name,*
> *I am there in the midst of them."*
> *Matthew 18:20 NKJV*

The enemy knows the promise of Christ concerning operating within a unit. It knows all too well two or more gathered ensures His presence. The enemy must avoid this at all costs. It knows efforts will be thwarted immediately when we gather together. Our coming together is critical to Kingdom success. We were redeemed to be gathered before Him. We are gathered together in Him.

> *"Though one may be overpowered by another, two can*
> *withstand him. And a threefold cord is not quickly broken."*
> *Ecclesiastes 4:12 NKJV*

These warrior units do not have to be large in number. The smaller ones are sometimes most effective. The smaller the unit of individuals, the more likely the warriors will connect with each other. They tend to bond and really expose their weaknesses to each other in order for the forging process to take place. Lowering the guard is essential to this strengthening process. For a muscle to become stronger, it must be stretched, broken down and weakened. The process of growth and repair demands it. Muscles go through a period of tearing down and building up to become stronger, just like the warrior. This can only be accomplished in an environment of trust and common purpose.

The small unit must provide respect and edification to its members. The warriors must develop a trust for each other. We must work toward transparency to expose our fears, shortcomings and weaknesses for the sharpening process. The rough spots on the blade will get identified, revealed and polished out. There will be sparks, flashes and flying shards. It will cause some issues of pain and trauma. We must undergo the refining process to create a divine weapon for God's Kingdom. It will require divine intervention to develop divine warriors.

Our natural man will want us to flee from this process. Our natural man will want us to succumb to our insecurities. The natural man will want us to give in to excuses and fears. It is at this point where the Lionheart Warrior is set apart. We long to be stronger. We love to be purified by the fire of discipline. We love the result of being sharpened because we know we will be much more effective against God's enemy. Lionheart Warriors embrace the refining process, because it manifests the King's power in us individually and in our unity. We must begin gathering together and initiate the process.

When putting our units together, the ideal situation is finding and setting aside weekly meeting times to train. Warriors need to study, pray and discuss their personal areas of operations. They need opportunity to share successes and failures. Understand, these gatherings can be accomplished any number of ways. With advancements in technology, meetings can be done traditionally or over social media platforms. Using these types of technology means there is no limit to the distance between warriors. Modern schedules are jammed packed full of events and obligations. This is no excuse for lack of commitment to the unit. We understand all kinds of excuses will come up to prevent these gatherings, but we know to push the issue and commit to the task.

Every organization needs a representative to take charge and push the agenda. We need to assign a unit leader. One who is gifted with leadership and has a heart for the other warrior's development. This leader will need to organize and keep the group on task and topic. A leader needs to be humble and wise, someone who can inspire and encourage all the warriors, not just a select few, someone who can delegate and motivate others to assist in their duties. This person does not need to be a scholar, but have a sincere love for the King and His kindred. The leader will organize the meetings and insure there is content covered. They do not have to be the content creator, but must possess the ability to delegate and hold the unit accountable to follow the refining process.

These warrior gatherings must be centered on God's mission in and around the warriors' lives. There must be accountability and support toward pursuing victories in all the warriors' AOs. Once again, we need to get to the point where we are willing to express our frustrations and expose our shortcomings to become stronger. We need to be in a place where we can fight the flesh's influence to project façades of superiority and the expressing of false bravado. Warriors need to be about truth. No one benefits from falsehood and fantasy in war. Being real is the only way to obtain true strength and power in Christ.

When these groups are utilized correctly, it will act as a force multiplier in the Lionheart Warrior's life. Creating a sense of connection and combined purpose inspires us to push to new heights of achievement. We will find an element of personal motivation to succeed like never before. We will not only be inspired and strengthened in our journey, but we will stay inspired and experience true empowerment from the Lord. We will develop a sense of unity that can only come through a community of like-minded warriors seeking a common end. Small unit identity and culture will spring board us toward victory in areas of our lives where we only knew defeat and frustration before. God has

designed us for relationship, thus assigning us to groups for the furtherance of His glory. Unity will be established through receiving His love
and then pouring it out into the others.

> *"A new commandment I give to you, that you love one*
> *another; as I have loved you, that you also love one another.*
> *By this all will know that you are My disciples, if you have*
> *love for one another."*
> *John 13:34-35 NKJV*

We will be known by our love for one another and our ability to
bear one another's burdens, thus falling in the footsteps of our Master
and Lord Jesus Christ.

May God be praised by our gathering in unity.

CHAPTER 25
STAY IN THE FIGHT

"Finally, my brethren, be strong in the Lord and in the power of His might."–Ephesians 6:10 KJV

As we bring this discussion to a conclusion, it is important we go back over some of the truths we have discussed. I have always enjoyed books that provide a nice little recap to all the vital points the author was trying to share. I suppose, as an author, you run the risk of the reader simply scanning the last chapter of your book and getting the general gist of the subject and therefore not purchasing the work. My chief concern is this particular perspective on the Christian life needs to be taught and therefore utilized.

We started this adventure trying to get a basic understanding of what exactly a Lionheart Warrior looks like. We wanted to understand that supernatural longing and draw inside of us to something greater than ourselves—that call to arms and adventure that causes those who are lost to build false kingdoms and potentially destroy everything around them. We understand this internal drive for purpose was placed inside of us and can only be fulfilled in our Creator. He is the only answer to all our longings. He alone is the solution to all our plaguing problems. More specifically, the answer is found in His Son, Jesus Christ.

We now understand all this is only possible through a relationship based in trusting faith in Christ. In that relationship alone is where we can reach our true purpose and true potential. Through the power of His saving works on the cross, we can expect to live a life of true significance and power. Without Him, we continue to be doomed to a life of inner chaos, shallowness and despair. At best, we can learn to numb it all through pointless strivings that never truly satisfy.

We understand, that without Him, we are separated from the love and care of God in a rebellious fallen state. In that state, we are at war with the only one who can give us peace—waging a moment-by-moment fight with Him in our flesh and seeking to raise ourselves and our desires above His, looking to glorify ourselves and our wills above His own. In doing that, we are blinded to His desires for relationship and fellowship with us. Being spiritually dead and lost, we are allied with the chief enemy of God's glory, the devil. Satan and the fallen angels have been waging an all-out war from the very beginning, their aim is to subvert and divert glory from the King of Kings. They seek to build up anything and everything in opposition to His reign. In doing that, they are in a constant quest to undermine His will.

The enemy has set up a counter-kingdom, a world system. Over the course of human history, this system feeds its destructive agenda. It empowers and equips fallen man in his own personal journey for glory. Through temptation and facilitation, the world guides and equips the flesh of man to go against the King in all his dealings. The world system sets up authorities and powers that govern the fallen world. It protects the enemy's agenda and constantly re-enforces it. Only through the redemptive work of Jesus is its power broken and the captives set free.

God sent His only son to live the perfect life we should have lived and set the stage for our redemption. He was arrested, charged and executed for crimes He personally did not commit. He was perfect and sinless in all His dealings. He did not deserve death, but died, none the less. It was a cosmic tragedy that rocked all of the created order.

He remained dead three days fulfilling countless biblical prophecies and on that third day rose from the dead. In doing that, He provided a way for humanity to be freed from their sinful rebellious state. He provided a way for those who received His sacrifice by faith to place their sin on Him in His death. By doing that in faith, we receive Christ's righteousness in exchange—a transfer of attributes. In transferring our sins past, present and future upon Jesus on the cross, we were punished through him. Divine justice was served once and for all. We were freed from the burden of having to account and pay for our own rebelliousness. As a free gift, grace was extended to us unmerited, all to show the love of God for us. A people He longed to restore to Himself.

> *Through a supernatural act of God, mankind was given the most precious gift, life eternal.*

In receiving the gift of salvation and declaring Jesus as King of Kings, we were given His righteousness. We were made new. We were made to be like Him in His perfect state. We were made co-heirs of His kingdom. We were made to be like Him. Through a supernatural act of God, mankind was given the most precious gift, life eternal. Life as it was meant to be. All received by faith in the One who gives. As new creations are now empowered to follow after His ways. We are now free to live a life we were meant to live. We are now able to reach our full potential in Christ.

God as our King, we become warriors for His cause. We become warriors for His kingdom. We are given hearts of a lion. We are given the One who has the heart of a lion. Jesus resides in us. The Lionheart King. He comes to live inside of us. He comes to provide us with power of purpose. He transforms us into Lionheart Warriors. We become His bearers of glory. We become His mighty force for the spreading of His kingdom.

Each Lionheart Warrior is given areas over which to take charge. Each are given responsibilities to uphold. These areas are vital to the Kingdom agenda and must be cultivated and protected on a daily basis. It is only through constant connection and reliance on the power of God that His warriors can accomplish their mission. We must grow closer to Him daily. We must study His word and be connected with His other warriors in order to overcome the enemy. Our enemy is ever vigilant in seeking our destruction.

We, Lionheart Warriors have been empowered by the Lord's Spirit to make adjustments, gain insights and move into those areas God has given us. We must never succumb to our old ways of doing things, but must do them the King's way. We must be on constant lookout for the ways of the enemy and must not fight this war the world's way. Our weapons and warfare are not of this world, but of the other. We use the armor of God to stand up to the enemy. We utilize all the tools provided. While looking to the Lord for our strength, we saturate our lives in prayer and thanksgiving. The Lord champions our cause as we strive to lift up the Son. God secures the victory. In seeking His Kingdom first, our every need is fully met. Through trust and reliance, we walk after the Spirit He gave us.

Since we have been promised to never be forsaken or abandoned by Him, we know we never operate alone. We operate in His love. After receiving His love, we turn around and spread His love to those who are lost and hurting. Taking His redemptive message, we seek out those living lives of desperation and condemnation. We share the love of God and His plan for salvation. We expand God's Kingdom through fighting off the enemy and rescuing as many lost and enslaved souls as possible.

By the prompting and power of God's Holy Spirit, we take back from the enemy those who belong to the King. Heaven rings out in glorious praise as each one is rescued in victory. We remain ever vigilant and steadfast to stand firm in His strength while fighting the enemy. Ultimately, we Lionheart Warriors know there will be a day when the King will return to the battlefield to secure the victory and declare peace throughout the land.

> "Therefore you also be ready, for the Son of Man is coming
> at an hour you do not expect."
> Matthew 24:44 NKJV

"For the Son of Man will come in the glory of His Father with His angels, and then He will reward each according to his works."
Matthew 16:27 NKJV

May we be found waiting and worthy.

Stay in the Fight!

To God be all the glory for ever and ever!

Amen.

APPENDIX

O nce the book is read and the warrior sees the necessity to invest in their training, it is important to develop an attack plan going forward. Conceptual recommendations were laid out in the book, but there is a need to provide some additional suggestions for training in this appendix section. Below you will find 3 basic items: The Lionheart Warrior Creed, a recommended verse study and a link to get further access to Lionheart Warrior resources.

It is my prayer that you use not only the information you read in the book, but also the resources that follow here. May God bless your mission going forward. Grace and Peace to you in the name of The Lionheart Warrior King Jesus Christ. Amen

The Lionheart Warrior Creed

I will deny myself, take up my cross and follow Christ daily. (Matt. 16:24)

I have been crucified with Him, it is no longer I who live, but Christ lives in me. (Gal. 2:20)

The life I live in the flesh, I live by faith in the Son of God, who loved me and gave Himself for me. (Gal. 2:20)

I will seek first His Kingdom and His righteousness in my life, trusting Him for all my provisions. (Matt. 6:33)

I will be strong in the Lord and the power of His might knowing through Him I can do all things. (Eph. 6:10, Phil. 4:13)

I will put on the full armor of God, so that I may stand firm in the evil day. (Eph. 6:13)

For His is the Kingdom and the power and the Glory for ever and ever. (Matt. 6:13)

Amen.

Suggested Verse Studies

Peace
Philippians 4:4-7, Isaiah 9:6, Isaiah 26:3, Isaiah 26:12,
1 Peter 5:7, John 14:27, John 16:33, Matthew 6:33 Ephesians 2:14

Prayer
1 Timothy 2:8, Philippians 4:6, Psalm 102:17, Jeremiah 29:11-13,
Psalm 145:18
1 John 5:14-15, Romans 12:2, John 14:12-14, Mark 11:22-24, James
4:3, Romans 8:26

Armor of God
2 Corinthians 10:3-5, Ephesians 6:10-20, 1 Thessalonians 5:8, 2
Corinthians 6:7
Hebrews 4:12, Isaiah 59:17, Isaiah 11:5, Isaiah 52:7, Romans 10:15,
Romans 13:12-14

Spirit
Ezekiel 36:26-27, Ephesians 6:12, Psalm 51:10, John 3:5,
Ephesians 3:16-17
1 John 4:13, 2 Timothy 1:7, Romans 8:6 , Romans 8:11, Romans 8:15,
Romans 8:16 Galatians 5:16

Mind

Genesis 3, Exodus 13:17, Romans 7:23, 1 Peter 1:13, Psalm 101:3, Philippians 2:2-8

Philippians 4:8, Romans 8:5-7, Colossians 3:2, 2 Corinthians 10:5, Romans 12

Body

Genesis 3:19, 1 Corinthians 6:19-20, 1 Corinthians 3:16-17, Romans 12:1-2, Galatians 2:20

1 Corinthians 10:31, 1 Timothy 4:8

Marriage

James 1:27, Malachi 2:16, Genesis 2:18-25, Matthew 19:4-6, Psalm 146:9

Exodus 22:22, Deuteronomy 14:29, Jeremiah 3:1,8,14, Ephesians 5:22-32

Colossians 3:19, 1 Peter 3:7, 17

Children

Genesis 4:1-8, Deuteronomy 6:4-9, Ephesians 6:4, Colossians 3:21, Proverbs 3:11

Proverbs 22:6, Psalms 127:3-5

Social Circle

Mark 12:29-31, John 13:34-35, Romans 12:10, Romans 15:2, 1 Corinthians 10:24, Proverbs 17:17, Proverbs 18:24

Galatians 6:2-10, Colossians 3:13, 1 Thessalonians 5:11

Career

Genesis 2:15, 1 Corinthians 10:31, Psalm 90:17, Proverbs 16:3, Proverbs 12:11

Proverbs 12:24, Proverbs 13:4, 1 Timothy 5:8, 2 Timothy 2:6, 3 John 1:2

THE LIONHEART WARRIOR RESOURCES

To get more information about upcoming events, courses and projects, visit us on the web at www.thelionheartwarrior.com .

Stay in the Fight and God Bless!

CPSIA information can be obtained
at www.ICGtesting.com
Printed in the USA
FFHW022145251119
56106170-62176FF